D1304272

taste.
CUPCAKES

Over 100 mouth-watering recipes

igloo

igloo

Published in 2012
by Igloo Books Ltd
Cottage Farm
Sywell
NN6 0BJ

www.igloo-books.com
Copyright © 2011 Igloo Books Ltd

All rights reserved. No part of this publication may be reproduced,
stored in a retrieval system,or transmitted in any way or by any means,
electronic, mechanical, photocopying, recording or otherwise,
without the prior written permission of the publisher.

B044 0312
2 4 6 8 10 9 7 5 3 1
ISBN: 978-0-85780-322-1

Food photography and recipe development: Stockfood, The Food Image Agency
Front and back cover images © Stockfood, The Food Image Agency

Printed and manufactured in China.

contents.

Indulgent	6
Simple	58
Celebration	112
Children's	164

introduction.

There is something magical about taking a fresh batch of cupcakes from the oven and smelling that wonderful aroma that fills the house.

A freshly baked cupcake brings a sense of comfort and there is nothing better than sharing your baked goods at celebrations and special occasions. This book is packed full of delicious, versatile sweet treats that are simple to make.

The recipes that follow are split into easy sections, so you can find the right cupcake to suit any occasion. There is everything from simple treats to spectacular and indulgent cupcakes, as well as cakes for celebrations and great ideas for fun cupcakes for kids.

The best place to start is with the recipes. The key to your baking success is being properly prepared, so take your time to read the instructions and ensure you have everything you need.

Here are a few tips to help you prepare:

Ingredients

Using fresh, organic ingredients will create the best possible taste, but don't worry if those products aren't available, your cupcakes will still be delicious! Unless otherwise specified, your ingredients should be at room temperature when you start. Butter should be soft, but not melted and try to use unsalted butter where possible. Eggs should be large and preferably free range. Check the type of sugar specified; use caster (superfine) sugar where a type of sugar is not mentioned and remember that light brown, dark drown and muscavado are all different and produce very different results.

Always sift dry ingredients, such as flour and icing sugar; this not only removes lumps but also aerates the flour or icing sugar and it makes it easier to mix, which produces a lighter sponge.

Measurement

If you're a beginner, make sure you measure your ingredients. Stick to using all metric, or all imperial measurements, this saves any confusion later on. Judgement comes with experience, so once you get the hang of measuring you will be able to improvise if scales aren't available. When measuring liquids, make sure you use a jug that is transparent, such as a plastic or glass jug, this will give you more accurate measurements.

Mixing

Make sure you have a mixing bowl big enough to easily combine all of your ingredients. Electric whisks are great for whisking egg whites and for creaming butter and sugar together; they speed up the mixing process, but are by no means necessary. You can whisk cream, or egg whites by hand – all you need is patience and a strong wrist! Hand whisks and spoons are great for mixing ingredients, but also come in handy if you need to smooth out any lumps, or fold ingredients in gently.

Baking

Use the correct size pans for your mixture. Always preheat your oven before you start mixing the ingredients, so that when you put your mixture into the oven it is an even temperature. Remember, every time you open the oven door to check the cake, you will let cool air into the oven and the temperature inside will fluctuate, affecting cooking times and quality. To test if a cupcake is done, insert a toothpick: if it comes out clean, it is cooked. When cupcakes first come out of the oven they are quite fragile, so always leave them to cool completely before decorating.

Decorating

Decorating your cupcakes really is the icing on the cake! This is where you can be as creative as you like. You can experiment with different types of icing, from buttercream to ganache, gel, chocolate and everything in between.

A palette knife is the best utensil for icing your cakes. For best results, heat your knife in hot water and wipe it dry before icing – if you have the time, repeat this for every stroke. You can also use a piping bag and nozzle, working in circular motions from the outside of the cake inwards.

Tip: if you don't have a piping bag, you can cut the corner of a freezer bag for the same effect.

Storage

Cupcakes are always best eaten the day they are made, however, you can make extra and freeze what you don't need immediately. You can also store them in an airtight container, to keep for a few days.

The wide range of exciting recipes that follow are selected to ensure that they will suit beginners and experts alike, so you can create spectacular cupcakes for every occasion.

indulgent.

Meringue cupcakes

Prep and cook time: 45 minutes
makes: 8

Ingredients:
110 g | 4 oz | ½ cup unsalted butter
110 g | 4 oz | ½ cup caster (superfine) sugar
2 eggs
110 g | 4 oz | 1 cup self-raising flour
1 tsp baking powder
1 lemon, finely grated zest
2 tbsp lemon juice

For the meringue:
2 egg whites
50 g | 2 oz | ¼ cup caster (superfine) sugar

Method:
Preheat the oven to 190°C (165° fan), 375F, gas 5 and place paper cases in a bun tin

Beat the butter and sugar in a mixing bowl until soft and creamy. Gradually beat in the eggs until smooth. Sift in the flour and baking powder and gently stir into the mixture with the lemon zest and juice until blended. Spoon the mixture into the paper cases.

For the meringue topping, whisk the egg whites until they stand in soft peaks. Gradually whisk in the sugar until the mixture is stiff.

Spoon the meringue on top of the cake mixture, swirling the mixture into peaks. Bake for 20-25 minutes until the meringue is crisp and golden. Allow to cool on a wire rack.

Giant cream cupcakes

Prep and cook time: 40 minutes
makes: 4

Ingredients:
5 eggs, separated
150 g | 5 oz sugar
1 tsp vanilla extract
1 pinch salt
150 g | 5 oz | 1 ¼ cups self-raising flour

For the cream:
250 ml | 8 ½ fl. oz | 1 cup cream
1 tbsp icing (confectioners') sugar
50 g | 2 oz dark (plain)
chocolate, melted
12 chocolate curls

Method:
For the cupcakes, heat the oven to 180°C (160° fan) 350F, gas 4 and place 4 large paper cases in a muffin tin.

Whisk the egg yolks with the sugar and vanilla until fluffy. In a clean bowl, whisk the egg whites with the salt until stiff and fold into the egg yolk-sugar mixture until smooth.

Sift the flour into the mixture and fold in gently until just combined. The mixture will be lumpy.

Pour the mixture into the paper cases and bake for 25-30 minutes. Test with a wooden toothpick, if it comes out clean, the cakes are done. Cool the cupcakes in the tins for 5 minutes then place on a wire rack to cool completely.

To make the cream, whisk the cream with the icing sugar until thick. Put into a piping bag and pipe onto each cupcake.

Drizzle with melted chocolate and decorate with chocolate curls.

Rum and ginger cupcakes

Prep and cook time: 45 minutes
makes: 12

Ingredients:
175 g | 6 oz | ¾ cup soft butter
175 g | 6 oz | 1 ¼ cup icing
(confectioners') sugar
3 egg yolks
2 eggs
2 tbsp rum
10 g | ½ oz freshly grated ginger
100 g | 3 ½ oz plain (all-purpose) flour
75 g | 2 ½ oz | ½ cup ground walnuts
1 tsp baking powder
1 pinch ground cinnamon
1 pinch salt

To decorate:
4 tbsp golden syrup
12 walnuts
3 figs, quartered

Method:
For the cupcakes, heat the oven to 180°C (155° fan), 350F, gas 4 and place 12 paper cases in a bun tin.

Cream the butter and 100g of the icing sugar until white and fluffy. Beat in the eggs, rum, ginger and remaining sugar until fluffy.

Mix the flour with the walnuts, baking powder, cinnamon and salt. Stir into the wet mixture until smooth and blended.

Spoon the mixture into the paper cases and bake for 25 minutes until risen and springy to the touch. Remove from the oven and cool in the tins for 5 minutes, then place on a wire rack to cool completely.

Heat the golden syrup in a small pan until bubbling, and then spoon a little on top of each cake and decorate with the fig quarters and walnuts.

Buttercream and raspberry cupcakes

Prep and cook time: 35 minutes
makes: 12

Ingredients:
175 g | 6 oz | ¾ cup butter
175 g | 6 oz | ¾ cup sugar
1 tsp vanilla extract
4 eggs, beaten
175 g | 6 oz | 1 ½ cups self-raising flour

For the buttercream:
75 g | 3 oz unsalted butter
175 g | 6 oz | 1 ¼ cups icing
(confectioners') sugar
1 tsp vanilla extract

To decorate:
12 raspberries

Method:
For the cupcakes, heat the oven to 180°C, (155° fan), 350F, gas 4. Place paper cases in a 12 hole bun tin.

Cream the butter and sugar in a mixing bowl until light and fluffy. Stir in the vanilla and gradually beat in the eggs. Sift in the flour and gently fold into the mixture until combined.

Spoon the mixture into the paper cases and bake for 20 minutes until golden and risen. Leave the cupcakes in the tins for 5 minutes and then place on a wire rack to cool completely.

For the buttercream, beat the butter in a bowl until soft. Sift in the icing sugar and beat well. Stir in the vanilla. Spoon the icing into a piping bag. Pipe a whirl of buttercream onto each cupcake and top with a raspberry.

Chocolate ginger cupcakes

Prep and cook time: 45 minutes
makes: 20

Ingredients:
150 g | 5 oz dark (plain)
chocolate, chopped
225 ml | 7 ½ fl. oz | 1 cup cream
1 tsp vanilla extract
1 tsp ground cinnamon
1 tsp ground ginger
225 g | 8 oz | 1 cup caster
(superfine) sugar
200 g | 7 oz unsalted butter
3 eggs, separated
225 g | 8 oz | 2 cups plain
(all-purpose) flour
3 tbsp cocoa powder
2 tsp baking powder

For the ginger buttercream:
225 g | 8 oz | 1 cup unsalted butter
450 g | 1 lb icing (confectioners') sugar
50 g | 2 oz stem ginger, finely chopped
75 g | 2 ½ oz crystallised (candied)
ginger, finely chopped

Method:
For the cupcakes, heat the oven to 190°C (170° fan) 375F, gas 5 and place 20 paper cases in bun tins.

Heat the chocolate and cream in a bowl over a pan of simmering water and stir until the chocolate has melted. Remove from the heat and stir in the vanilla and spices.

Beat the sugar and butter in a mixing bowl until light and creamy. Gradually beat in the egg yolks until blended.

Sift the flour, cocoa and baking powder into the egg yolk mixture, followed by the melted chocolate and stir until just combined. The mixture will be slightly lumpy.

Whisk the egg whites until stiff and gently fold them into the mixture. Spoon the mixture into the paper cases and bake for 20 minutes until firm to the touch. Cool the cupcakes in the tins for 5 minutes then place on a wire rack to cool completely.

For the buttercream, beat the butter in a bowl until soft. Sift in the icing sugar and stem ginger and beat well.

Spread the buttercream on top of the cool cakes, then sprinkle with crystallised ginger.

Vanilla-iced chocolate cupcake

Prep and cook time: 30 minutes
makes: 12

Ingredients:
110 g | 4 oz | ½ cup butter, softened
110 g | 4 oz | ½ cup sugar
2 eggs
110 g | 4 oz | 1 cup self-raising flour
1 tsp baking powder
1 tbsp cocoa powder

For the icing:
110 g | 4 oz | ½ cup butter
225 g | 8 oz | 1 ½ cups icing
(confectioners') sugar
1 tsp vanilla extract
2 tbsp cream
50 g | 2 oz | ¼ cup grated chocolate

Method:
For the cupcakes, heat the oven to 170°C (150° fan) 325F, gas 3 and place 12 paper cases in a bun tin.

Put all the cake ingredients into a mixing bowl and beat well with an electric whisk or wooden spoon until combined.

Spoon the mixture into the paper cases and bake for about 20 minutes until risen and firm. Cool the cupcakes on a wire rack.

For the icing, beat the butter until soft and sift in the icing sugar. Add the vanilla and beat well. Beat in just enough cream to form a creamy consistency. Spread thickly on top of the cakes and sprinkle with grated chocolate to decorate.

Boston cream cupcakes

Prep and cook time: 3 hours
makes: 12

Ingredients:
For the custard filling:
220 ml | 7 ½ fl. oz | ⅞ cup milk
2 tbsp cornstarch (cornflour)
3 egg yolks
75 g | 2 ½ oz sugar
1 tbsp unsalted butter
1 tsp vanilla extract
1 pinch of salt

For the cupcakes:
150 g | 5 ½ oz unsalted butter, softened
300 g | 10 ½ oz | 1 ¼ cups caster
(superfine) sugar
1 tsp vanilla extract
6 egg yolks
350 g | 3 cups plain (all-purpose) flour
2 ½ tsp baking powder
¼ tsp salt

For the chocolate icing:
140 ml | 5 fl. oz | ⅝ cup cream
200 g | 7 oz dark (plain)
chocolate, chopped

Method:
To make the custard filling, whisk together half the milk with the cornflour until smooth. Add the egg yolks and whisk until blended then set aside.

Combine the remaining milk with the sugar in a pan and heat to a boil over medium heat, stirring occasionally. Remove from the heat and whisk half the milk mixture into the egg yolk mixture. Return the mixture to the pan and bring to a boil. Simmer gently for 1 minute, whisking constantly until slightly thickened.

Remove from the heat and whisk in the butter, vanilla extract and salt. Pour into a bowl, cover and refrigerate for at least 2 hours until thickened and completely cool.

For the cupcakes, heat the oven to 180°C (155° fan), 350F, gas 4 and grease a 12 hole muffin tin with butter.

Beat the butter and sugar with an electric whisk until light and fluffy. Gradually beat in the vanilla and egg yolks until the mixture is smooth. Gradually whisk in the flour, baking powder and salt and beat until smooth.

Set aside 400 ml of the mixture. Spoon the remaining mixture into the muffin tins. Make a well in the centre of each filled cupcake, using the back of a teaspoon. Add about 2 tablespoons custard filling. Completely cover the filling with reserved mixture.

Bake for 20-25 minutes until the tops are golden brown and set. Cool in the tins for 10 minutes. Remove from the tins and place on a wire rack to cool completely.

For the icing, heat the cream in a pan and bring to a boil. Remove from the heat and add the chocolate. Whisk until the chocolate is completely melted, then allow it to cool and thicken.

Spread the icing over the top of each cupcake and leave to set.

Cupcakes with ice-cream

Prep and cook time: 30 minutes
makes: 12

Ingredients:
125 g | 4 ½ oz plain (all-purpose) flour
250 g | 10 oz condensed milk
1 egg
½ tsp vanilla extract
75 g | 3 oz butter, softened
1 ½ tsp baking powder

To decorate:
1 block, vanilla ice cream
1 block, raspberry ripple ice cream
12 sugar cones
24 raspberries

Method:
Heat the oven to 180°C (160° fan) 350F, gas 4 and grease a 12 hole cupcake tin with butter.

Put all the ingredients for the cupcakes in a mixing bowl and beat with an electric whisk or wooden spoon for 2-3 minutes until pale and fluffy.

Spoon the mixture into the cupcake tins and bake for 15-18 minutes until golden and springy to the touch. Allow the cupcakes to cool in the tins for 5 minutes, then remove and place on a wire rack to cool completely.

To decorate, cut the ice cream blocks into 12 small slices. Place a vanilla slice on each cupcake and a raspberry ice cream slice on top. Attach a sugar cone in the top and decorate with raspberries, then serve immediately.

Toffee cupcakes

Prep and cook time: 40 minutes
makes: 12

Ingredients:
225 g | 8 oz | 2 cups plain
(all-purpose) flour
110 g | 4 oz | ½ cup caster
(superfine) sugar
2 tsp baking powder
a pinch of salt
1 egg, beaten
150 ml | 5 fl. oz | ⅔ cup milk
50 ml | 2 fl. oz sunflower oil
1 tsp vanilla extract

For the toffee cream:
110 g | 4 oz | ½ cup sugar
2 tbsp water
a pinch of salt
400 ml | 13.5 fl. oz | 1 ⅔ cups cream

For the caramel sauce:
250 g | 9 oz | 1 ¼ cups caster
(superfine) sugar
4 tbsp water
150 ml | 5 fl. oz | ⅔ cup cream
50 g | 2 oz | ¼ cup butter

Method:

For the cupcakes, heat the oven to 200°C (175° fan) 400F, gas 6. Arrange 12 paper cases in a 12 hole bun tin.

Sift the flour, sugar, baking powder and salt into a mixing bowl. Whisk together the egg, milk, oil and vanilla. Stir in the dry ingredients until combined. Spoon the mixture into the paper cases and bake for 20 minutes until golden and risen. Cool in the tin for 5 minutes then place on a wire rack to cool.

For the toffee cream, heat the sugar, water, and salt in a pan over medium heat, stirring once, until the sugar is dissolved. Continue cooking, but do not stir, until the sugar turns a golden amber, and then remove from the heat.

Slowly pour the cream into the pan. Reheat the pan gently, stirring until it has combined. Pour the toffee cream into a mixing bowl and leave it to cool. Chill for 40 minutes until cold, stirring occasionally.

For the caramel sauce, put the sugar into a heavy-based frying pan and stir in the water. Heat gently, making sure you do not stir or the sugar will crystallise, until it has all dissolved. Increase the heat and gently boil for 4-5 minutes until golden brown. Remove from the heat, and carefully stir in the cream and butter. Pour the caramel sauce into a jug or bowl and leave to cool.

Whisk the toffee cream until soft peaks form. Spoon the mixture into a piping bag and pipe on top of the cold buns, then drizzle with caramel sauce.

Chocolate meringue cupcakes

Prep and cook time: 1 hour 40 minutes
makes: 12

Ingredients:
175 g | 6 oz | 1 cup ground
hazelnuts (cobnuts)
175 g | 6 oz | 1 ¼ cups icing
(confectioners') sugar
75 g | 2 ½ oz | ¾ cup plain
(all-purpose) flour
5 egg whites
50 g | 2 oz | ½ cup dark (plain)
chocolate, grated

For the chocolate meringue:
3 egg whites
125 g | 4 ½ oz caster (superfine) sugar
1 tbsp cocoa powder
⅛ tsp cream of tartar

For the chocolate icing:
110 g | 4 oz | ½ cup butter
2 tbsp cocoa powder, sifted
150 g | 5 oz | 1 cup icing
(confectioners') sugar

Method:
For the cupcakes, heat the oven to 200°C (180° fan) 400F, gas 6. Place 12 paper cases in a bun tin.

Put the hazelnuts in a mixing bowl and sift in the icing sugar and flour. Stir in the egg whites and grated chocolate. Spoon the mixture into the paper cases and bake for 15-20 minutes until golden. Leave the cakes in the tins for 5 minutes then place on a wire rack to cool completely.

Reduce the oven temperature to 180°C (160°fan) 350F, gas 4.

For the chocolate meringue, line a large baking tray with non-stick paper. Whisk the egg whites and cream of tartar in a bowl until soft peaks form, then gradually whisk in the sugar, 1 tablespoon at a time, until stiff and glossy. Sift in the cocoa powder and gently fold into the egg whites.

Spoon small rounds of the meringue onto the baking tray. Put them into the oven, then immediately turn the heat down to its lowest setting. Bake for about 45 minutes -1 hour, until crisp on the outside. Place on a wire rack to cool.

For the icing, beat the butter and cocoa powder until combined. Gradually sift in the icing sugar and beat well until smooth. Spread a little onto each cake and top with a disc of meringue.

Mini cherry cupcakes

Prep and cook time: 45 minutes
makes: 24

Ingredients:
75 g | 3 oz butter
75 g | 3 oz caster (superfine) sugar
2 eggs, beaten
½ tsp almond extract
75 g | 2 ½ oz | ¾ cup self-raising flour
75 g | 2 ½ oz glacé (candied)
cherries, chopped

To decorate:
110 g | 4 oz icing (confectioners') sugar
2-3 tsp hot water
24 whole fresh cherries

Method:

For the cupcakes, heat the oven to 180°C (160° fan) 350F, gas 4. Place 24 paper cases in a small cupcake tin.

Beat the butter and sugar until light and fluffy. Gradually add the eggs, a little at a time and beat well.

Sift in the flour and gently fold into the mixture. Stir in the almond extract and candied cherries.

Spoon the mixture into the paper cases and bake for 12-15 minutes until golden and springy to the touch. Place them on a wire rack to cool completely.

For the icing, sift the icing sugar into a bowl and stir in enough hot water to make a thick paste.

Spread a little icing on each cake and top with a fresh cherry.

Black Forest cupcakes

Prep and cook time: 45 minutes
makes: 12

Ingredients:
150 g | 5 oz butter
110 g | 4 oz | ½ cup sugar
1 tsp vanilla extract
2 eggs, beaten
200 g | 7 oz | 1 ¾ cups plain
(all-purpose) flour
25 g | 1 oz cocoa powder
2 tsp baking powder
120 ml | 4 ½ fl. oz milk
50 g | 2 oz | ½ cup grated dark
(plain) chocolate

For the topping:
90 ml | 3 fl. oz kirsch
200 ml | 7 oz | ⅞ cup cream
12 tbsp cherry compote

To decorate:
50 g | 2 oz | ½ cup dark (plain)
chocolate, roughly chopped

Method:
For the cupcakes, heat the oven to 180°C (155° fan) 350F,
gas 4, and grease a 12 hole bun tin with butter.

Beat the butter with an electric whisk until smooth.
Gradually beat in the sugar and vanilla until very creamy.
Beat the eggs into the mixture until smooth.

Sift the flour, cocoa and baking powder together and
then gently fold into the milk until combined. Stir in the
grated chocolate.

Spoon the mixture into the tins and bake for about
25 minutes until risen. Remove from the tins and cool on a
wire rack. Once cooled, cut the cakes in half horizontally
and sprinkle with kirsch.

For the topping, whisk the cream until thick and spoon into
a piping bag. Pipe half of the cream onto the cake bottom
halves and top with a little compote. Sprinkle with chocolate
shavings. Place the remaining cake halves on top and
decorate with the rest of the whipped cream, cherry compote
and chocolate. Serve chilled.

Ice-cream cupcakes

Prep and cook time: 45 minutes
makes: 12

Ingredients:
2 eggs
250 ml | 8 ½ fl. oz | 1 cup milk
125 ml | 4 fl. oz | ½ cup sunflower oil
200 g | 7 oz sugar
1 tsp vanilla extract
450 g | 1 lb | 4 cups plain
(all-purpose) flour
4 tsp baking powder
a pinch of salt
12 scoops vanilla ice-cream, softened

To decorate:
225 g | 8 oz | 2 cups raspberries

Method:
For the cupcakes, heat the oven to 200°C (180° fan) 400F, gas 6 and grease a 12 hole cupcake tin with butter.

Beat the eggs, milk, oil, sugar and vanilla in a mixing bowl until smooth. Sift in the flour, baking powder and salt and stir until just combined. The mixture will be lumpy.

Spoon the mixture into the cupcake tins and bake for 20-25 minutes until risen, golden and firm. Cool in the tins for 5 minutes then place on a wire rack to cool completely.

Cut each cupcake into 3 horizontal slices with a sharp knife. Place half a scoop of ice cream on the flat base, top with the middle cupcake slice, then the other half scoop of ice-cream. Add the top of the cupcake. Repeat with all the cupcakes and ice-cream. Freeze if not serving immediately.

To decorate, sift a little icing sugar over each cupcake and decorate with raspberries.

Tiramisu cupcakes

Prep and cook time: 30 minutes
makes: 12

Ingredients:
110 g | 4 oz | ½ cup butter, softened
110 g | 4 oz | ¾ cup light brown sugar
110 g | 4 oz | 1 cup self-raising flour
1 tbsp cocoa powder
1 tbsp espresso coffee powder
2 large eggs
1-2 tbsp milk

To decorate:
300 ml | 10 fl. oz | 1 ⅓ cups cream
30 g | 1 oz icing (confectioners') sugar
60 g | 2 oz cocoa powder

Method:
For the cupcakes, heat the oven to 180°C (160° fan) 350F, gas 4. Place 12 paper cases cupcake tin.

Beat all the cake ingredients in a mixing bowl until smooth and creamy. Add more milk if the mixture is too stiff. Spoon the mixture into the paper cases and bake for 18-20 minutes until springy to the touch. Allow the cakes to cool in the tins for 5 minutes, then place on a wire rack to cool completely.

For the icing, whisk the cream and icing sugar until thick. Spoon the mixture into a piping bag and pipe on top of the cakes. Lightly sift cocoa powder over the top just before serving.

Chocolate cupcakes

Prep and cook time: 35 minutes
makes: 10

Ingredients:
110 g | 4 oz | ½ cup butter
110 g | 4 oz | ¾ cup light brown sugar
2 eggs, beaten
150 g | 5 oz | 1 ¼ cups plain
(all-purpose) flour
1 tsp baking powder
25 g | 1 oz cocoa powder
110 ml |3 ½ fl. oz milk

For the icing:
75 ml | 2 ½ fl. oz | ⅓ cup cream
175 g | 6 oz dark (plain) chocolate
50 g | 2 oz | ¼ cup butter
edible silver baubles

Method:
For the cupcakes, heat the oven to 190°C (170° fan) 375F, gas 5 and place 10 paper cases in a bun tin.

Beat the butter in a mixing bowl until soft and light. Beat in the sugar and beat until light and fluffy. Beat in the eggs, gradually until well blended. Sift in the flour, baking powder and cocoa and fold in gently until incorporated, then stir in the milk.

Spoon the mixture into the paper cases and bake for 25 minutes until firm to the touch. Leave the cakes in the tins for 5 minutes then place on a wire rack to cool completely.

For the icing, bring the cream to a boil in a pan. Remove from the heat and add the chocolate. Stir until melted and then add in the butter. Continue to stir until the mixture is smooth and shiny. Chill until it is thick enough to pipe.

Put the mixture into a piping bag and pipe on top of each cake and decorate with silver baubles.

Macadamia nut cupcakes

Prep and cook time: 35 minutes
makes: 12

Ingredients:
200 g | 7 oz | 1 ¾ cups plain
(all-purpose) flour
2 ½ tsp baking powder
110 g | 4 oz | ½ cup sugar
½ tsp salt
175 g | 6 oz | ¾ cup macadamia
nuts, chopped
180 ml | 6 fl. oz | ¾ cup milk
80 ml | 2 ½ fl. oz | ⅓ cup sunflower oil
1 egg

For the icing:
175 g | 6 oz | 1 ¼ cups icing
(confectioners') sugar
4-5 tsp hot water
pink food dye

Method:

For the cupcakes, heat the oven to 200°C (180° fan) 400F, gas 6 and grease a 12 hole cupcake tin with butter.

Mix the flour, baking powder and sugar in a mixing bowl. In a small bowl, mix the milk, oil and egg. Stir into the dry ingredients with the nuts until just combined. The mixture will be lumpy.

Spoon the mixture into the cupcake tins and bake for 20 minutes until golden brown and risen. Cool the cupcakes in the tins for 5 minutes then place on a wire rack to cool completely.

For the icing, sift the icing sugar into a bowl and gradually stir in the water and a few drops of food dye. Drizzle the icing over the top of the cooled cakes.

Advocaat cupcakes

Prep and cook time: 50 minutes
makes: 12

Ingredients:
25 g | 1 oz cocoa powder
100 ml | 3 fl. oz boiling water
50 g | 2 oz | ¼ cup butter
100 g | 3 ½ oz | ½ cup light brown sugar
1 egg
75 g | 2 ½ oz | ¾ cup plain
(all-purpose) flour
½ tsp bicarbonate of soda
(baking soda)
a pinch of baking powder

For the advocaat cream:
220 ml | 7 fl. oz | ⅞ cup cream
45 g | 1 ½ oz icing (confectioners') sugar
120 ml | 4 ½ fl. oz advocaat

For the chocolate cream:
140 ml | ⅝ cup cream
200 g | 7 oz dark (plain)
chocolate, chopped

Method:
For the cupcakes, heat the oven to 190°C (165° fan) 375F, gas 5. Place the paper cases in a 12 hole bun tin.

Whisk the cocoa and boiling water to a smooth paste, and the set the paste aside to cool.

Beat the butter and sugar until light and smooth, then beat in the egg. Sift in the flour, bicarbonate of soda and baking powder and fold in gently with the cocoa paste.

Spoon the mixture into the paper cases and bake for 15-20 minutes until risen and springy to the touch. Place on a wire rack to cool.

For the advocaat cream, whisk all the ingredients together until smooth and thick. Put the mixture into a piping bag and pipe on top of the cool cakes. Chill while you make the chocolate topping.

For the chocolate cream, heat the cream in a pan and bring it to boiling point. Remove from the heat and add the chocolate, stirring while it melts. Allow the cream to cool and thicken.

Carefully spoon the chocolate over the top of the advocaat cream and leave to set.

Espresso cupcakes with mascarpone cream

Prep and cook time: 40 minutes
makes: 12

Ingredients:
110 g | 4 oz | 1 cup self-raising flour
110 g | 4 oz | ¾ cup light brown sugar
110 g | 4 oz | ½ cup butter, softened
2 eggs, beaten
2 tbsp cold strong black espresso

For the mascarpone cream:
175 g | 6 oz | ¾ cup butter
350 g | 12 oz | 2 ¼ cups icing
(confectioners') sugar
225 g | 8 oz | 1 cup mascarpone

Method:

For the cupcakes, heat the oven to 180°C (155° fan), 350F, gas 4 and place 12 paper cases in a bun tin.

Sift the flour and baking powder into a mixing bowl and stir in the sugar. Beat in the eggs, and espresso, beating until combined.

Spoon the mixture into the paper cases and bake for about 20 minutes until risen and springy to the touch. Leave in the tins for 5 minutes then place on a wire rack to cool completely.

For the mascarpone cream, beat the butter until soft, then sift in the sugar. Gradually beat in the mascarpone until smooth and creamy. Spoon some of the cream on top of each cupcake and sprinkle with cinnamon.

Strawberry cupcakes

Prep and cook time: 2 hours 35 minutes
makes: 10

Ingredients:
2 eggs
110 g | 4 oz | ½ cup caster
(superfine) sugar
50 ml | 2 fl. oz cream
1 tsp vanilla extract
110 g | 4 oz | 1 cup self-raising flour
½ tsp baking powder
50 g | 2 oz | ¼ cup butter, melted
icing (confectioners') sugar
sliced strawberries

For the strawberry mousse:
250 g | 9 oz strawberries, sliced
25 g | 1 oz sugar
140 g | 5 oz mini marshmallows
200 ml | 7 fl. oz | ⅞ cup cream

Method:
For the strawberry mousse, put the strawberries into a pan with 100 ml water and the sugar. Increase the heat to boiling point and simmer for about 3 minutes until the strawberries are soft. Remove from the heat and mash until pulpy. Stir the marshmallows into the hot pulp until they dissolve. Stir and leave to cool.

Whisk the cream until it forms soft peaks, but is not stiff. Fold the cream into the cooled strawberry mixture, then spoon into a bowl and chill for 2 hours.

For the cupcakes, heat the oven to 180°C (160° fan) 350F, gas 4, then lightly grease a 10 hole bun tin with butter.

Beat the eggs and sugar until light, then beat in the cream and vanilla. Sift over the flour and baking powder and fold in lightly, followed by the butter.

Fill the bun tins ¾ full with the mixture and bake for 12-15 minutes until golden. Test with a wooden toothpick, if it comes out clean, the cakes are done. Remove from the oven and leave to cool in the tins for 5 minutes, then turn the cakes onto a wire rack to cool completely.

Split each cold cupcake into 3 horizontal slices, using a sharp knife. Place a spoonful of the strawberry mousse on one layer and spread thickly. Top with a layer of cupcake and spread another spoonful of mousse and top with the final layer of cake. Chill until ready to serve.

To decorate, sift a little icing sugar over the top layer just before serving and top with sliced strawberries.

Chocolate sauce cupcakes

Prep and cook time: 30 minutes (+12 hours freezing time)
makes: 4

Ingredients:
100 g | 3 ½ oz dark (plain) chocolate
2 large eggs
75 g | 2 ½ oz caster (superfine) sugar
60 g | 2 oz unsalted butter
45 g | 1 ½ oz plain (all-purpose)
flour, sifted
1 tbsp cream

For the chocolate sauce:
50 g | 2 oz dark (plain) chocolate
1 tbsp cream

Method:
For the cakes, butter 4 ramekins or deep muffin tins and dust with a little sugar.

Melt the chocolate in a bowl over simmering water and leave to cool slightly. Whisk the eggs and sugar together until thick and pale.

Stir the butter into the melted chocolate until well combined. Gradually stir into the egg mixture, followed by the flour and the cream, until everything is well blended. Pour the mixture into the ramekins and freeze overnight.

Heat the oven to 190°C (170° fan) 375F, gas 5. Bake from frozen for 12-15 minutes, until the cakes are cooked, but the centre is still liquid. Remove from the oven and allow the cakes to cool for 2 minutes.

For the chocolate sauce, heat the chocolate and cream in a heatproof bowl over a pan of simmering water until the chocolate has almost melted. Remove the bowl from the pan and stir until the chocolate has melted, allowing it to cool slightly.

Place the cakes on serving plates and spoon the extra chocolate sauce on top of the cakes. Serve warm with ice-cream or crème fraiche.

Chocolate ganache cupcakes

Prep and cook time: 1 hour 10 minutes
makes: 24

Ingredients:
400 g | 14 oz | 3 ¾ cups plain
(all-purpose) flour
200 g | 7 oz butter
100 g | 3 ½ oz | ⅞ cup icing
(confectioners') sugar
1 egg yolk, beaten
1 tsp ground cinnamon
1 pinch salt

For the chocolate ganache:
125 ml | 4 fl. oz | ½ cup cream
250 g | 9 oz | 10 oz dark (plain)
chocolate, chopped
2 tbsp rum
2 tbsp butter

To decorate:
24 raspberries

Method:
For the cupcakes, heat the oven to 180°C (155° fan) 350F, gas 4 and grease a 24 hole mini-bun tin.

Mix the flour, sugar, cinnamon and salt in a mixing bowl. Rub in the butter with your fingertips until the mixture resembles breadcrumbs.

Stir in the enough egg yolk to form a dough and knead it quickly and form into a ball. Wrap the dough in cling film and refrigerate for 30 minutes.

Roll out the pastry on a floured surface about 5 mm / ¼ " thick. Cut out circles about 8 cm / 3 " in diameter and line the bun tins with them. Prick the base of the pastry cases with a fork.

Bake for 10-15 minutes until golden brown. Leave in the tins for a few minutes to cool, then place on a wire rack to cool completely.

For the chocolate ganache, heat the cream in a pan and increase the heat to boiling point. Immediately remove from the heat and pour over the chocolate. Stir until the chocolate has melted, then stir in the rum. Add the butter gradually and stir until it is smooth. Allow the mixture to cool until it is thick enough to pipe. Spoon or pipe the ganache into the cool pastry cases and top each with a raspberry.

Bee sting cupcakes

Prep and cook time: 45 minutes
makes: 18

Ingredients:
110 g | 4 oz | ½ cup butter
110 g | 4 oz | ½ cup sugar
1 egg, separated
110 ml | 4 oz honey
250 g | 9 oz | 2 ¼ cups plain
(all-purpose) flour
1 tsp bicarbonate of soda (baking
soda)
60 ml | 2 fl. oz milk
300 ml | 10 fl. oz | 1 ⅓ cups cream

To decorate:
125 ml | 4 oz | ½ cup honey
75 g | 3 oz | ¾ cup flaked almonds

Method:
For the cupcakes, heat the oven to 200°C (165° fan) 400F, gas 6. Grease a 18 hole bun tin with a butter.

Beat the butter and sugar together in a mixing bowl until light and fluffy. Beat in the egg yolk then slowly add the honey, beating well.

Sift in the flour and bicarbonate of soda and gently stir into the mixture until just combined. Add enough milk to create a soft dropping consistency. In a separate bowl, whisk the egg white until stiff and fold it into the mixture until everything is smooth.

Spoon the mixture into the bun tin and bake for 25 minutes until golden. Leave in the bun tin for 5 minutes then place on a wire rack to cool. Whisk the cream until it is stiff.

Cut each cake in half horizontally. Spoon the whipped cream on each flat half and drizzle with honey.

Replace the tops of the cakes and drizzle with more honey and flaked almonds to top each cupcake.

Coconut cupcakes

Prep and cook time: 45 minutes
makes: 12

Ingredients:
175 g | 6 oz | ¾ cup butter
225 g | 8 oz | 1 cup caster
(superfine) sugar
2 eggs
1 tsp vanilla extract
225 g | 8 oz | 2 cups plain
(all-purpose) flour
2 tsp baking powder
125 ml | 4 fl. oz | ½ cup natural
(plain) yoghurt
175 g | 6 oz | 2 cups desiccated
(flaked) coconut

To decorate:
175 g | 6 oz | 1 ¼ cups icing
(confectioners') sugar
2 tbsp lemon juice
1 tsp hot water
desiccated (flaked) coconut, toasted

Method:
For the cupcakes, heat the oven to 180°C (155° fan), 350F, gas 4 and place 12 large paper cases in a 12 hole tin.

Cream the butter and sugar in a mixing bowl until light and fluffy, then beat in the eggs and vanilla.

Sift in the flour and baking powder and gently fold into the mixture with the yoghurt, until well combined. Stir in the coconut.

Spoon the mixture into the paper cases and bake for 25-30 minutes until golden and springy to the touch. Leave in the tins for 5 minutes then place on a wire rack to cool.

For the icing, sift the icing sugar into a bowl and gradually stir in the lemon juice and water until smooth.

Spoon a little icing onto each cake and smooth level with a palette knife and sprinkle with the toasted coconut.

Hazelnut fancy cupcakes

Prep and cook time: 45 minutes
makes: 4

Ingredients:
1 vanilla pod (bean)
125 ml | 4 ½ fl. oz | ½ cup milk
60 g | 2 oz butter
60 g | 2 oz plain (all-purpose) flour
4 eggs, separated
75 g | 3 oz dark (plain) chocolate,
melted and cooled
30 g | 1 ¼ oz ground roasted hazelnuts
50 g | 2 oz | ¼ cup sugar
Frangelico hazelnut liqueur

To decorate:
150 g | 5 oz dark (plain)
chocolate, chopped
3 tbsp chocolate hazelnut spread
75 ml | ⅓ cup cream
100 g | 3 ½ oz whole hazelnuts, roasted

Method:
For the cupcakes, heat the oven to 180°C (160° fan) 350F, gas 4, then butter 4 individual pudding tins and sprinkle with sugar.

Cut the vanilla pod in half and scrape out the seeds. Heat the milk, vanilla pod and the vanilla seeds in a pan.

Melt the butter in another pan. Add the flour and stir until the paste is smooth.

Remove the vanilla pod from the milk and pour into the butter paste. Simmer for 3 minutes, stirring occasionally. Pour the mixture into a mixing bowl and let it cool slightly. Stir in 2 egg whites, followed by the egg yolks, one after the other, stirring the mixture until smooth.

Stir in the melted chocolate and ground hazelnuts. Whisk the two remaining egg whites with the sugar until stiff. Stir ¼ of the egg whites into the chocolate mixture, then fold the remaining egg white in carefully until incorporated.

Spoon the mixture into the tins. Place the tins in an ovenproof dish half-filled with water and bake for 25- 30 minutes, test with a wooden toothpick, if it comes out clean, the cakes are done.

Turn the cakes out of the tins and allow them to cool completely. Pour a little nut liqueur over the cakes, according to taste.

For the icing, melt the chocolate in a heatproof bowl over a pan of simmering water. Allow it to cool slightly then stir in the chocolate hazelnut spread and the cream. Leave the mixture to cool and firm up. Spread the icing over the cakes and sprinkle roasted hazelnuts over the top.

Chocolate cupcakes

Prep and cook time: 50 minutes
makes: 12

Ingredients:
200 g | 7 oz plain (all-purpose) flour
1 tsp baking powder
½ tsp bicarbonate of soda
(baking soda)
110 g | 4 oz | ½ cup caster
(superfine) sugar
225 g | 8 oz courgettes (zucchini),
peeled and finely grated
2 eggs
175 ml | 6 fl. oz | ¾ cup sunflower oil
175 g | 6 oz dark (plain)
chocolate, melted

To decorate:
225 g | 8 oz | 1 cup butter
450 g | 16 oz | 3 cups icing
(confectioners') sugar
1 tsp vanilla extract
red rose petals

Method:
For the cupcakes, heat the oven to 180°C (160° fan) 350F, gas 4 and grease a 12 hole cupcake tin with butter.

Sift the flour, baking powder and bicarbonate of soda into a mixing bowl. Mix in the sugar and grated zucchini.

Whisk together the eggs and oil. Stir into the dry ingredients, followed by the warm, melted chocolate.

Spoon the mixture into the cupcake tins and bake for 30-35 minutes until well risen and springy to touch. Cool in the tins for 5 minutes then place on a wire rack to cool.

For the buttercream, beat the butter until soft and creamy. Sift in the icing sugar and beat well and stir in the vanilla.

Spread the buttercream over the top of the cakes and decorate with rose petals.

simple.

Carrot cupcakes

Prep and cook time: 45 minutes
makes: 12

Ingredients:
2 eggs
175 g | 6 oz | ¾ cup caster
(superfine) sugar
150 ml | 6 fl. oz | ⅔ cup sunflower oil
200 g | 7 oz self-raising flour
2 tsp mixed spice
1 tsp ground cinnamon
2 carrots, coarsely grated
1 tsp vanilla extract
1 orange, finely grated zest

For the cream icing:
50 g | 2 oz clotted cream
225 g | 8 oz | 1 ½ cups icing
(confectioners') sugar, sifted
2 tsp vanilla extract
2-3 tbsp very hot water

Method:

For the cupcakes, heat the oven to 180°C (155° fan), 350F, gas 4 and place 12 medium paper cases in bun tins.

Put the eggs, sugar and oil in a large bowl and beat with an electric whisk for 2-3 minutes until light and fluffy. Gently fold in the flour, spices, grated carrot, vanilla extract and the orange zest, until thoroughly combined.

Spoon the mixture into the paper cases and bake for 20-25 minutes until risen and golden brown. Remove from the oven and cool on a wire rack.

For the cream icing, beat the clotted cream, icing sugar and vanilla with the hot water until thick, smooth and spreadable. Spread icing on top of each cake and decorate with edible flowers (optional).

Chocolate cupcakes with sugar pearls

Prep and cook time: 55 minutes
makes: 12

Ingredients:
110 g | 4 oz | ½ cup butter
200 g | 7 oz | 1 ¼ cup dark brown sugar
1 egg, beaten
½ tsp vanilla extract
50 g | 2 oz dark (plain)
chocolate, melted
100 g | 3 ½ oz plain (all-purpose) flour
½ tsp bicarbonate of soda
(baking soda)
125 ml | 4 fl. oz | ½ cup boiling water

To decorate:
200 ml | ⅞ cup cream
100 g | 3 ½ oz dark (plain)
chocolate, chopped
100 g | 3 ½ oz milk chocolate,
chopped pink and white sugar pearls

Method:
For the cupcakes, heat the oven to 180°C (160° fan) 350F, gas 4 and place 12 paper cases in a cupcake tin.

Cream the butter and sugar in a mixing bowl until light and soft. Gradually beat in the egg and vanilla. Stir in the melted chocolate. Sift in the flour and bicarbonate of soda and stir into the mixture alternately with the boiling water until the mixture is smooth.

Pour into the paper cases and bake for 25-30 minutes until risen, test with a wooden toothpick, if it comes out clean, the cakes are done. Cool in the tins for 5 minutes then place on a wire rack to cool completely.

For the icing, heat the cream in a pan to boiling point. Immediately remove from the heat and stir in the chocolate until melted. Leave to cool and thicken for a few minutes.

Put a spoonful of icing on each cake and spread with a palette knife. Sprinkle with sugar pearls before the icing sets.

Buttercream cupcakes

Prep and cook time: 40 minutes
makes: 12

Ingredients:
225 g | 8 oz | 2 cups self-raising flour
175 g | 6 oz | ¾ cup caster
(superfine) sugar
1 lemon, finely grated zest
3 eggs
100 ml | 3 ½ fl. oz plain yoghurt
175 g | 6 oz | ¾ cup butter, melted

For the buttercream:
50 g | 2 oz | ¼ cup unsalted butter
100 ml | 3 ½ fl. oz cream
½ tsp vanilla extract
350 g | 12 oz | 2 ½ cups icing
(confectioners') sugar
pink food dye
blue food dye
12 sugar flowers

Method:
For the cupcakes, heat the oven to 180°C (160° fan) 350F, gas 4 and place paper cases in a 12 hole cupcake tin.

Mix the flour, sugar and lemon zest together in a mixing bowl. Beat the eggs with the yoghurt, then pour into the dry ingredients with the melted butter. Mix together until just combined. The mixture will be slightly lumpy.

Spoon the mixture into the paper cases and bake for 20-25 minutes until risen and firm to the touch. The cakes will be quite pale on top. Cool for 5 minutes in the tins, then place on a wire rack to cool completely.

For the buttercream, beat the butter until soft and creamy. Beat in the cream and vanilla until blended. Sift in the icing sugar and beat until smooth. Put half the mixture into a bowl and add a few drops of pink food dye. Add blue food dye to the other bowl. Spread the buttercream generously on top of the cool cakes and decorate with sugar flowers.

Lemon cakes

Prep and cook time: 40 minutes
makes: 10

Ingredients:
75 g | 2 ½ oz butter, melted
1 egg, lightly beaten
175 ml | 6 fl. oz | ¾ cup plain yoghurt
1 lemon, juice and finely grated zest
250 g | 9 oz | 2 ¼ cups plain
(all-purpose) flour
1 tbsp baking powder
150 g | 5 oz sugar

To decorate:
250 g | 2 cups icing
(confectioners') sugar
60 ml | 2 fl. oz lemon juice
1 tsp hot water

Method:
For the cupcakes, heat the oven to 180°C (160° fan) 350F, gas 4.
Grease 10 holes of a cupcake tin with butter.

Combine the butter, egg, yoghurt, lemon juice and zest in
a mixing bowl. Sift in the flour, baking powder and sugar.

Spoon the mixture into the tins, almost to the top. Bake for
25 minutes until golden and risen. Leave the cupcakes to
cool in the tins for 5 minutes, then place on a wire rack to
cool completely.

For the icing, sift the icing sugar into a bowl and gradually stir
in the lemon juice and water until smooth. Spoon the icing over
the cupcakes, allowing it to run down the sides.

Pink cupcakes

Prep and cook time: 35 minutes
makes: 12

Ingredients:
225 g | 8 oz | 1 cup butter
225 g | 8 oz | 1 cup caster
(superfine) sugar
4 eggs, beaten
110 g | 4 oz | 1 cup self-raising flour
1 tsp rosewater
1 tbsp cream

For the icing:
175 g | 6 oz | 1 ¼ cups icing
(confectioners') sugar
3-4 tsp hot water
pink food dye

Method:

For the cupcakes, heat the oven to 180°C (155° fan), 350F, gas 4. Place 12 large paper cases in a 12 hole bun tin.

Beat the butter and sugar until light and fluffy. Gradually beat in the eggs until blended. Sift in the flour and beat well. Stir in the rosewater and cream.

Spoon the mixture into the paper cases and bake for 20-25 minutes until golden and risen. Cool in the tin for 5 minutes then place on a wire rack to cool completely.

For the icing, mix the icing sugar with the hot water and a few drops of pink food dye, to make a thick, smooth icing. Spoon the icing into a piping bag. Ice the cakes and decorate with sugar sprinkles.

Sugar flower cupcakes

Prep and cook time: 45 minutes
makes: 12

Ingredients:
225 g | 8 oz | 2 cups plain
(all-purpose) flour
110 g | 4 oz | ½ cup caster
(superfine) sugar
2 tsp baking powder
1 egg, beaten
150 ml | 5 fl. oz | ⅔ cup milk
50 ml | 2 fl. oz sunflower oil
1 tsp vanilla extract

To decorate:
450 g | 16 oz white sugarpaste
icing (confectioners') sugar
blue food dye
yellow food dye
1-2 tbsp apricot jam (jelly), warmed

Method:
Heat the oven to 180°C (160° fan) 350F, gas 4. Place 12 paper cases in a cupcake tin.

Sift the flour, sugar and baking powder into a mixing bowl. Whisk together the egg, milk, oil and vanilla, then stir into the dry ingredients until combined.

Spoon the mixture into the paper cases and bake for 20 minutes until golden and risen. Cool in the tins for 5 minutes then place on a wire rack to cool completely.

To decorate, divide the sugarpaste in half. Knead a few drops of blue food dye into one half until evenly coloured. Cut off ¼ of the white sugarpaste and knead in a few drops of yellow food dye until evenly coloured.

Roll out the blue sugarpaste thinly on a surface dusted with icing sugar. Cut out rounds slightly smaller than the diameter of the cakes. Brush the tops of the cakes with a little apricot jam and attach to the cakes.

Roll out the remaining white sugarpaste thinly on a surface dusted with icing sugar. Cut out 8 petals for each cake. Mark a line down the centre of each petal with a sharp knife. Attach to the blue sugarpaste with a dab of apricot jam.

Roll small pieces of the yellow sugarpaste into 12 small rounds for the centre of the flower and attach in the centre of the petals with a little apricot jam.

Roll the scraps of the white sugarpaste into tiny balls and place on the yellow centres of the flowers and on the blue sugarpaste.

Lemon cupcakes

Prep and cook time: 40 minutes
makes: 12

Ingredients:
110 g | 4 oz | ½ cup butter
110 g | 4 oz | ½ cup caster
(superfine) sugar
110 g | | 4 oz | 1 cup self-raising flour
2 eggs, beaten
1 pinch salt
1 lemon, finely grated zest

To decorate:
225 g | 8 oz | 1 ½ cups icing
(confectioners') sugar
3 tbsp lemon juice
1-2 tsp hot water
yellow food dye
2 lemons, grated zest

Method:
For the cupcakes, heat the oven to 180°C (160° fan) 350F, gas 4.
Place 12 paper cases in a cupcake tin.

Beat the butter and sugar in a mixing bowl until pale and fluffy.
Gradually beat in the eggs until the mixture is smooth. Fold in
the flour, salt and lemon zest until blended.

Spoon the mixture into the paper cases. Bake the cakes for
15-20 minutes, until golden and springy to the touch, and allow
them to cool on a wire rack.

For the icing, sift the icing sugar into a bowl and gradually stir in
the lemon juice and enough hot water until thick and smooth.

Divide the icing in half and add a few drops of food dye to
one half. Spoon a little yellow icing on half of the cakes and
smooth with a palette knife. Spread the remaining cakes
with white icing.

Scatter the lemon zest on top of the cakes before the
icing sets.

Chocolate raspberry cupcakes

Prep and cook time: 35 minutes
makes: 12

Ingredients:
200 g | 7 oz butter
200 g | 7 oz dark (plain) chocolate
200 g | 7 oz light brown sugar
100 ml | 7 tbsp hot water
2 eggs, beaten
1 tsp vanilla extract
250 g | 9 oz | 2 ½ cups self-raising flour

For the icing:
110 g | 4 oz | ½ cup butter, softened
175 g | 6 oz | 1 ¼ cups icing
(confectioners') sugar
55 g | 2 oz cocoa powder
1-2 tbsp milk

To decorate:
12 raspberries

Method:

For the cupcakes, heat the oven to 160°C (135° fan), 325F, gas 3 and place 12 paper cases in a bun tin.

Melt the butter, chocolate, sugar and hot water together in a large pan on a low heat, stirring occasionally, then set aside to cool slightly.

Stir the eggs and vanilla into the chocolate mixture. Sift the flour into a mixing bowl, then stir in the chocolate mixture until smooth.

Spoon the mixture into the paper cases and bake for 20 minutes until firm and golden. Cool in the tins for 5 minutes then place on a wire rack to cool completely.

For the icing, beat the butter in a large bowl until soft. Sift in half of the icing sugar and beat until smooth. Sift in the remaining icing sugar and cocoa powder and stir until combined. Add 1 tablespoon of the milk and beat until creamy. Beat in more milk if necessary to loosen the icing. Spoon a little icing on top of each cake and decorate with a fresh raspberry.

Butterfly buns

**Prep and cook time: 40 minutes
makes: 12**

Ingredients:
2 eggs
110 g | 4 oz | 1 cup self-raising flour
½ tsp baking powder
110 g | 4 oz | ½ cup butter, softened
110 g | 4 oz | ½ cup sugar

To decorate:
175 ml | 6 fl. oz | ¾ cup cream
icing (confectioners') sugar

Method:
For the buns, heat the oven to 170°C (150° fan) 325F, gas 3 and place 12 paper cases in a bun tin.

Put all the ingredients for the cakes into a mixing bowl and beat until well combined. Spoon the mixture into the paper cases and bake for 20-30 minutes until golden and springy to the touch. Cool the buns on a wire rack.

Carefully cut round the tops of the cakes with a cutter or sharp knife and remove the top of each cake. Slice the tops in half to form 2 wings.

To decorate, whisk the cream until thick but not stiff. Spoon the cream into a piping bag. Pipe a whirl onto each cake and press the wings into the cream. Sift over a little icing sugar.

Vanilla and chocolate cupcakes

Prep and cook time: 45 minutes
makes: 12

Ingredients:
200 g | 7 oz | 1 ¾ cups self-raising flour
2 tsp baking powder
200 g | 7 oz butter, softened
4 eggs
200 g | 7 oz caster (superfine) sugar
45 ml | 1 ½ fl. oz milk
50 g | 2 oz ground almonds
1 tsp vanilla extract

To decorate:
200 g | 7 oz | 1 cup unsalted butter
250 g | 9 oz | 2 cups icing (confectioners') sugar
½ tsp vanilla extract
25 g | 1 oz dark (plain) chocolate, melted
50 g | 2 oz dark (plain) chocolate, coarsely grated
coloured sugar sprinkles

Method:

For the cupcakes, heat the oven to 180°C (160° fan) 350F, gas 4. Place 12 paper cases in a cupcake tin.

Put all the cake ingredients into a mixing bowl and whisk with an electric whisk until smooth. Alternatively, beat together with a wooden spoon until combined.

Spoon the mixture into the paper cases and bake for 20-25 minutes until golden and risen. Leave the cakes to cool for 5 minutes and then place on a wire rack to cool completely.

For the buttercream, beat the butter until soft. Sift in the icing sugar and beat well until smooth and creamy, then stir in the vanilla extract. Divide the mixture in half and stir the melted chocolate into one half. Beat well until blended.

Spread half of the cakes with vanilla buttercream and the rest of the cakes with chocolate buttercream. Sprinkle grated chocolate over the chocolate cupcakes and sugar sprinkles over the vanilla cupcakes.

Vanilla cupcakes

Prep and cook time: 55 minutes
makes: 20

Ingredients:
1 egg
50 g | 2 oz | ¼ cup sugar
110 ml | 3 ½ fl. oz milk
50 g | 2 oz | ¼ cup butter, melted
½ tsp vanilla extract
150 g | 5 oz | 1 ¼ cups plain
(all-purpose) flour
½ tbsp baking powder
a pinch of salt

For the icing:
225 g | 8 oz | 1 cup sugar
60 ml | 2 oz | ¼ cup water
¼ tsp cream of tartar
2 egg whites
1 tsp vanilla extract
10 glace (candied) cherries, halved

Method:
For the cupcakes preheat the oven to 200°C (180° fan) 400F, gas 6. Place 20 paper cases in a mini muffin tin.

Mix together the egg, sugar, milk, butter and vanilla in a mixing bowl until combined.

Sift in the flour, baking powder and salt and fold gently into the mixture until blended, but still slightly lumpy.

Spoon the mixture into the paper cases and bake for 12-18 minutes until well risen. Cool in the tins for 5 minutes then place on a wire rack to cool completely.

For the vanilla cream, heat the sugar, water and cream of tartar in a pan over a low heat until the sugar has dissolved completely. Bring the mixture to a boil on a low heat for 3 minutes until syrupy but not browned.

Whisk the egg whites and vanilla until you have soft peaks. Gradually pour in the hot syrup in a thin, steady stream, whisking constantly for about 10 minutes until the mixture is stiff and cool.

Spoon on top of the cakes and decorate with half a glace cherry.

Red velvet cupcakes

Prep and cook time: 35 minutes
makes: 12

Ingredients:
140 g | 5 oz | 1 ¼ cups self-raising flour
30 g | 1 oz cocoa powder
½ tsp bicarbonate of soda
(baking soda)
a pinch of salt
110 ml | 4 oz buttermilk
1 tsp white vinegar
½ tsp vanilla extract
1 tbsp red food dye
50 g | 2 oz | ¼ cup butter
175 g | 6 oz | ¾ cup caster
(superfine) sugar
1 egg

For the icing:
300 g | 10 ½ oz cream cheese (soft)
50 g | 2 oz | ¼ cup butter, softened
1 tsp vanilla extract
350 g | 12 oz | 2 ½ cups icing
(confectioners') sugar

Method:
For the cupcakes, heat the oven to 170°C (145° fan), 325F, gas 3. Place 12 paper cases in a bun tin.

Stir together the flour, cocoa, baking soda and salt in a mixing bowl. In another bowl mix the buttermilk, vinegar, vanilla and red food dye.

Beat the butter and sugar together until pale and creamy. Beat in the egg a little at a time. Mix in ⅓ of the flour mixture, followed by half the buttermilk mixture, then another third of the flour, the remaining buttermilk and finally the last of the flour mixture.

Spoon the mixture into the paper cases. Bake for 20 minutes, until risen and springy. Remove and cool on a wire rack.

For the icing, whisk all the ingredients together, then cover and chill for 1 hour before using. Spread or pipe the icing over the cakes.

Tea time cupcakes

Prep and cook time: 45 minutes
makes: 12

Ingredients:
110 g | 4 oz | ½ cup unsalted butter
110 g | 4 oz | ½ cup caster
(superfine) sugar
1 tsp vanilla extract
110 g | 4 oz | 1 cup self-raising flour
1 pinch of salt
1 tsp custard powder
2 eggs, beaten

For the buttercream:
140 g | 5 oz unsalted butter
250 g | 9 oz | 1 ¾ cups icing
(confectioners') sugar
pink food dye
½ tsp natural strawberry extract
½ tsp vanilla extract
coloured sugar sprinkles
pink and white sugar pearls

Method:
For the cupcakes, heat the oven to 180°C (160° fan) 350F, gas 4. Place 12 paper cases in a cupcake tin.

Cream the butter and sugar until light and fluffy and stir in the vanilla. Sift in the flour, salt and custard powder and lightly fold into the mixture alternately with the eggs until well blended.

Spoon into the paper cases and bake for 20-25 minutes until golden brown and springy to the touch.

For the buttercream, beat the butter in a bowl until light and creamy. Gradually sift in the icing sugar and beat well until smooth and then divide the mixture in half. Colour one half pink and stir in strawberry extract to your taste.

Beat the vanilla extract into the remaining buttercream. Put the buttercream into 2 piping bags and pipe on top of the cakes. Sprinkle with the sugar sprinkles and sugar pearls to decorate.

Apple cupcakes

Prep and cook time: 25 minutes
makes: 12

Ingredients:
110 g | 4 oz | ½ cup caster
(superfine) sugar
110 g | 4 oz | 1 cup self-raising flour
110 g | 4 oz | ½ cup butter, melted
2 eggs
1 apple, peeled and diced

To decorate:
icing (confectioners') sugar
mint leaves

Method:
For the cupcakes, heat the oven to 180°C (155° fan), 350F, gas 4, and grease a 12 hole bun tin with butter.

Whisk the eggs and sugar together in a mixing bowl until light and fluffy. Gently fold in the flour and butter, followed by the apple.

Pour the mixture into the bun tins and bake for 8-10 minutes, until golden brown and springy to the touch. Leave in the tins for 10 minutes to cool and then place on a wire rack to cool completely.

Sift over a little icing sugar just before serving and decorate with mint leaves.

Fairy cakes

Prep and cook time: 40 minutes
makes: 12

Ingredients:
2 eggs
110 g | 4 oz | 1 cup self-raising flour
½ tsp baking powder
110 g | 4 oz | ½ cup butter, softened
110 g | 4 oz | ½ cup sugar
1 tsp vanilla extract

For the icing:
175 g | 6 oz | 1 ¼ cups icing (confectioners') sugar
30 ml | 1 fl. oz lemon juice
1 tsp hot water
pink food dye

Method:
Preheat the oven to 170°C (145° fan), 325F, gas 3 and place 12 paper cases in a bun tin.

Put all the cake ingredients into a bowl and combine well. Spoon the mixture into the paper cases and bake for 25-30 minutes until golden and springy to the touch. Remove from the tin and place on a wire rack to cool.

For the icing, sift the icing sugar into a bowl and gradually stir in the lemon juice and hot water until smooth. Add pink food dye to deepen the colour you wish.

Spoon the icing onto each cake and smooth with a palette knife.

Cupcakes with sugar flowers

Prep and cook time: 30 minutes
makes: 12

Ingredients:
2 eggs
110 g | 4 oz | ½ cup caster
(superfine) sugar
50 ml | 2 oz | cream
1 tsp vanilla extract
110 g | 4 oz | 1 cup self-raising flour
110 g | 4 oz | ½ cup butter, melted

For the icing:
350 g | 12 oz | 2 ½ cups icing
(confectioners') sugar
1-2 tbsp hot water
pink food dye
green food dye

Method:

For the cupcakes, heat the oven to 180°C (155° fan), 350F, gas 4, and place paper cases in a 12 hole bun tin.

Whisk the eggs and sugar together in a mixing bowl until light and fluffy. Stir in the vanilla, and gently fold in the flour and butter.

Pour the mixture into the paper cases and bake for 8-10 minutes, until golden brown and well-risen. Leave in the tins for 10 minutes and then place on a wire rack to cool.

Sift the icing sugar into a bowl and stir in enough hot water to make a smooth, thick icing.

Divide the mixture into 3 bowls, and add a teaspoon of pink food dye to a bowl and a teaspoon of green to the other. Mix well and add more dye if desired.

Spread the icing over the top of the cupcakes and decorate with a sugar flower before the icing sets.

Cupcakes with pink buttercream

Prep and cook time: 30 minutes
makes: 12

Ingredients:
110 g | 4 oz | ½ cup butter, softened
110 g | 4 oz | ½ cup caster
(superfine) sugar
2 eggs
110 g | 4 oz | 1 cup self-raising flour
½ tsp baking powder
1 tsp lemon juice

For the buttercream:
140 g | 5 oz unsalted butter
350 g | 12 oz | 2 ½ cups icing
(confectioners') sugar
140 g | 5 oz | ⅔ cup crème fraiche
pink food dye

To decorate:
pink and white sugar pearls

Method:
For the cupcakes, heat the oven to 180°C (155° fan),
350F, gas 4 and place paper cases in a 12 hole bun tin.

Beat the butter and sugar in a mixing bowl until soft and light.
Beat in the eggs, a little at a time until well blended.
Gently stir in the flour and baking powder until well mixed.
Stir in the lemon juice.

Spoon the mixture into the paper cases and bake for
15 minutes until golden and springy to the touch.
Remove from the tin and cool on a wire rack.

For the buttercream, beat the butter until soft and creamy.
Sift in the icing sugar and crème fraiche and beat until
the mixture is thick and creamy. Stir in a few drops of
pink food dye.

Put a spoonful of buttercream on top of each cake and
decorate with sugar pearls.

Lemon cupcakes

Prep and cook time: 40 minutes
makes: 10

Ingredients:
225 g | 8 oz | 2 cups plain
(all-purpose) flour
2 tsp baking powder
150 g | 5 oz superfine (caster) sugar
1 egg, beaten
300 ml | 1 ⅓ cups plain yoghurt
1 tbsp finely grated lemon zest
75 g | 3 oz butter, melted

For the icing:
225 g | 8 oz | 1 cup crème fraiche
50 g | 2 oz | ½ cup icing
(confectioners') sugar, sifted
1 lemon, juice and zest

Method:
For the cupcakes, heat the oven to 180°C (155° fan) 350F, gas 4, and place 10 paper cases in a bun tin.

Sift the flour and baking powder into a mixing bowl and stir in the sugar.

In another bowl mix together the egg, yoghurt, lemon zest and melted butter. Stir into the dry ingredients until just mixed.

Spoon the mixture into the paper cases and bake for 25 minutes until golden and springy to the touch. Cool on a wire rack.

For the icing, put all the ingredients in a bowl and whisk with an electric whisk until thick and creamy. Cover and chill. Spread the icing over the cakes and sprinkle with lemon zest.

Fairy cakes

Prep and cook time: 40 minutes
makes: 12

Ingredients:
150 g | 5 oz butter
150 g | 5 oz | 1 cup icing
(confectioners') sugar
3 eggs
80 g | 2 ½ oz self-raising flour
50 g | 2 oz ground almonds
25 g | 1 oz cornflour (cornstarch)

To decorate:
250 g | 9 oz | 2 cups icing
(confectioners') sugar, sifted
2-4 tbsp water
pink food dye
edible silver baubles

Method:
Preheat the oven to 180°C (160° fan) 350F, gas 4. Place 12 paper cases in a small cupcake tin.

Beat the butter with the eggs and sugar until light and fluffy. Stir in the flour, ground almonds and cornflour.

Spoon the mixture into the paper cases and bake for about 15 minutes. Remove from the oven and leave them to cool slightly in the tins, and then place on a wire rack to cool completely.

To decorate, mix the icing sugar with water to make a thick icing. Divide the icing into 2 parts and colour half with pink food dye.

Coat the fairy cakes with one colour of icing and decorate by piping designs with the other colour, once set. You may need to thin the icing with a little water before piping. Decorate the fairy cakes with silver baubles and leave to set.

Iced fairy cakes

Prep and cook time: 35 minutes
makes: 12

Ingredients:
175 g | 6 oz | ¾ cup butter
175 g | 6 oz | ¾ cup caster
(superfine) sugar
1 tsp vanilla extract
3 eggs, beaten
175 g | 6 oz | 1 ½ cups self-raising flour

To decorate:
225 g | 8 oz | 1 ½ cups icing
(confectioners') sugar
1-2 tbsp hot water
pink food dye
desiccated (flaked) coconut
sugar flowers
coloured sugar sprinkles

Method:
Preheat the oven to 180°C (160° fan) 350F, gas 4 and place
12 paper cases in a cupcake tin.

Cream the butter and sugar in a mixing bowl until light
and fluffy and stir in the vanilla. Gradually beat in the eggs.
Sift in the flour and gently fold into the mixture until combined.

Spoon the mixture into the paper cases and bake for
20 minutes until golden and risen. Leave the cakes to
cool in the tins for 5 minutes, then place on a wire rack to
cool completely.

For the icing, sift the icing sugar into a bowl and gradually
stir in the hot water until smooth and thick. Put half of the icing
in another bowl and add a few drops of pink food dye.

Spoon icing onto each cake and smooth it with a palette knife.
Decorate with coconut, sugar flowers and coloured sprinkles
before the icing sets.

Vanilla cream cupcakes

Prep and cook time: 35 minutes
makes: 12

Ingredients:
100 g | 3 ½ oz | 1 cup
cornstarch (cornflour)
140 g | 5 oz | 1 ¼ cups plain
(all-purpose) flour
1 ½ tsp baking powder
200 g | 7 oz caster (superfine) sugar
¼ tsp salt
110 g | 4 oz | ½ cup butter, melted
2 eggs
100 ml | 3 ½ fl. oz milk
½ tsp vanilla extract

For the vanilla cream:
50 g | 2 oz | ¼ cup unsalted butter
100 ml | 3 ½ fl. oz milk
½ tsp vanilla extract
350 g | 12 oz | 2 ½ cups icing
(confectioners') sugar

To decorate:
75 g | 3 oz white chocolate,
coarsely grated

Method:

Preheat the oven to 160°C (135° fan), 300F, gas 2 and place 12 medium paper cases in a muffin tin.

Mix the cornstarch, flour, baking powder, sugar and salt in a mixing bowl. Whisk the butter, eggs, milk and vanilla together. Pour ⅓ of the egg-milk mixture into the flour mixture and stir gently. Add the remaining egg-milk mixture and stir until just combined. The batter will be quite thick.

Spoon the mixture into the paper cases and bake for 17-20 minutes until golden and firm to the touch. Leave the cupcakes in the tins for 10 minutes and then cool completely on a wire rack.

For the cream, beat the butter with an electric whisk for 2-3 minutes until fluffy. Mix in the milk and vanilla extract alternately with the icing sugar and whisk until the cream is light and fluffy.

Spread a thick layer of the cream over the cooled cupcakes and decorate with grated white chocolate.

Banana cupcakes

Prep and cook time: 40 minutes
makes: 12

Ingredients:
150 g | 5 oz butter
150 g | 5 oz sugar
150 g | 5 oz | 1 ¼ cups plain
(all-purpose) flour
50 g | 2 oz | ⅓ cup walnuts, chopped
1 tsp baking powder
2 ripe bananas
3 eggs

For the icing:
1 ripe banana
100 ml | 3 ½ fl. oz cream
30 g | 1 oz icing (confectioners') sugar
30 g | 1 oz cream cheese (soft)
1 tbsp lemon juice

To decorate:
coloured sugar sprinkles

Method:
For the cupcakes, heat the oven to 200°C (175° fan), 400F, gas 6 and place paper cases in a 12 hole cupcake tin.

Mash the bananas and then beat the eggs with the butter and sugar until well blended. Beat in the banana, then stir in the walnuts.

Sift in the flour and baking powder until just combined. Spoon the mixture into the paper cases and bake for about 25 minutes until golden and risen. Leave in the tins for 5 minutes and then allow them to cool completely on a wire rack.

For the icing, mash the banana and beat in the cream, icing sugar, cream cheese and lemon juice until thick and smooth.

Spread the topping on the cakes and decorate with sugar sprinkles.

Chocolate strawberry cream cakes

Prep and cook time: 40 minutes
makes: 12

Ingredients:
200 g | 7 oz plain (all-purpose) flour
25 g | 1 oz cocoa powder
1 tbsp baking powder
1 tsp ground cinnamon
110 g | 4 oz | ½ cup sugar
2 eggs
100 ml | 3 ½ fl. oz sunflower oil
225 ml | 7 ½ fl. oz | 1 cup milk

To decorate:
300 ml |10 fl. oz | 1 ⅓ cups cream
6 strawberries, halved

Method:
For the cupcakes, heat the oven to 200°C (180° fan) 400F, gas 6. Place 12 paper cases in cupcake tin.

Sift the flour, cocoa, baking powder and cinnamon into a mixing bowl and stir in the sugar. Whisk together the eggs and oil in a separate bowl until frothy, then slowly whisk in the milk.

Stir the wet ingredients into the dry ingredients until just blended. The mixture will be slightly lumpy.

Spoon the mixture into the paper cases and bake for 20 minutes until risen and springy to the touch. Cool in the tins for 5 minutes then place on a wire rack to cool.

To decorate, whisk the cream until thick. Spoon the cream onto the cupcakes, spreading it out with a palette knife. Place half a strawberry on top of the cream.

Raspberry cream cupcakes

Prep and cook time: 50 minutes
makes: 10

Ingredients:
2 eggs, beaten
75 g | 3 oz caster (superfine) sugar
240 ml | 8 fl. oz | 1 cup milk
100 ml | 3 ½ fl. oz sunflower oil
300 g | 10 oz | 2 ½ cups plain
(all-purpose) flour
3 tsp baking powder
¼ tsp salt

For the raspberry buttercream:
175 g | 6 oz | ¾ cup unsalted butter
350 g | 12 oz | 2 ¼ cups icing
(confectioners') sugar
45 g | 1 ½ oz seedless raspberry
jam (jelly)
pink food dye

To decorate:
10 sugar flowers

Method:
Preheat the oven to 200°C (175° fan), 400F, gas 6 and place 10 medium paper cases in a muffin tin.

Mix the egg, sugar, milk and oil in a mixing bowl. Sift in the flour, baking powder, salt and quickly mix until combined, be careful not to over mix the ingredients.

Spoon the mixture into the muffin cases. Bake for 30-35 minutes until well risen and golden. Cool the cupcakes on a wire rack.

For the raspberry buttercream, beat the butter until creamy and sift in the icing sugar and beat together until smooth. Stir in the raspberry jam and a few drops of pink food dye until the mixture is smooth and evenly coloured.

Spread the buttercream thickly over the cooled cakes and top with a sugar flower to decorate.

Raspberry bun cupcakes

Prep and cook time: 35 minutes
makes: 12

Ingredients:
250 g | 9 oz raspberries
250 g | 9 oz | 2 ¼ cups self-raising flour
50 g | 2 oz ground almonds
1 tsp baking powder
1 egg
200 ml | ⅞ cup cream
2 tbsp crème fraiche
120 g | 4 ½ oz sugar
2 tbsp raspberry liqueur
60 g | 2 ½ oz butter, melted
150 g | 5 oz marzipan, chopped

Method:
Preheat the oven to 180°C (160° fan) 350F, gas 4. Place 12 paper cases in a cupcake tin.

Set 12 raspberries aside for the decoration. Mix the remaining raspberries with the flour, almonds and baking powder.

Mix the egg with the cream, crème fraiche, sugar, liqueur and butter in a mixing bowl. Quickly stir in the flour mixture. Spoon half the mixture into the paper cases, sprinkle with the chopped marzipan, then spoon over the remaining mixture. Place a raspberry in the top of each bun.

Bake for 20-25 minutes until golden brown. Remove from the oven and leave in the tins for 5 minutes. Remove from the tins and allow the cupcakes to cool on a wire rack.

Chocolate raspberry cupcakes

Prep and cook time: 45 minutes
makes: 12

Ingredients:
100 g | 3 ½ oz plain (all-purpose) flour
1 tbsp baking powder
a pinch of salt
175 g | 6 oz | ¾ cup sugar
225 g | 8 oz | 1 cup butter
110 g | 4 oz dark (plain) chocolate
4 eggs, beaten
1 tsp vanilla extract
75 g | 2 ½ oz | ¾ cup chopped walnuts

To decorate:
175 g | 6 oz dark (plain) chocolate, chopped
175 ml | 6 fl. oz | ¾ cup cream
75 g | 3 oz dark (plain) chocolate, finely grated
raspberries

Method:
For the cupcakes, heat the oven to 200°C (180° fan) 400F, gas 6 and place 12 paper cases in a cupcake tin.

Sift the flour, baking powder and salt into a mixing bowl and stir in the sugar.

Melt the chocolate and butter in a heatproof bowl over a pan of simmering water. Remove from the heat and stir into the flour mixture.

Add the eggs and vanilla to the mixture and stir until only just combined, then stir in the walnuts.

Spoon the mixture into the paper cases and bake for 20-25 minutes, test with a wooden toothpick, if it comes out clean, the cakes are done. Cool the cakes in the tins for 5 minutes then place on a wire rack to cool.

For the icing, heat the chopped chocolate and cream in a pan over a low heat until melted and smooth. Allow to cool and thicken, then stir well.

Spoon the icing over the cupcakes and sprinkle with grated chocolate. Decorate with raspberries.

celebration.

Chocolate Christmas cupcakes

Prep and cook time: 35 minutes
makes: 12

Ingredients:
110 g | 4 oz | ½ cup butter, softened
110 g | 4 oz | ¾ cup light brown sugar
75 g | 3 oz self-raising flour
25 g | 1 oz cocoa powder, sifted
1 pinch of baking powder
2 eggs

For the chocolate ganache topping:
150 ml | 5 fl. oz | ⅔ cup cream
350 g | 12 oz dark (plain)
chocolate, chopped
50 g | 2 oz | ¼ cup butter

To decorate:
gold sugar sprinkles

Method:

For the cupcakes, heat the oven to 190°C (165° fan), 375F, gas 5. Place 12 paper cases in a bun tin.

Whisk together the butter, sugar, flour, cocoa, baking powder and eggs until smooth and blended.

Spoon the mixture into the paper cases and bake for 15 minutes until well risen and firm to the touch. Place on a wire rack and leave to cool.

For the chocolate ganache, heat the cream to a boil in a pan. Remove the pan from the heat and add the chocolate.
Stir until the chocolate has melted. Add the butter and stir until the mixture is smooth and glossy. Chill until the ganache is firm, but not hard.

Put the mixture into a piping bag and pipe on top of the cooled cakes. Scatter gold sugar sprinkles over the cupcakes.

Valentine's day chocolate cupcakes

Prep and cook time: 55 minutes
makes: 10

Ingredients:
110 g | 4 oz | ½ cup butter
75 g | 3 oz caster (superfine) sugar
30 g | 1 oz light brown sugar
2 eggs
150 g | 5 oz | 1 ¼ cups plain
(all-purpose) flour
1 tsp baking powder
25 g | 1 oz cocoa powder
120 ml | 4 oz | ½ cup milk
175 g | 6 oz | 1 cup chocolate chips

For the icing:
75 g | 3 oz dark (plain) chocolate
25 g | 1 oz butter
75 g | 3 oz | ½ cup icing
(confectioners') sugar
30 ml | 1 fl. oz warm water

To decorate:
150 g | 5 oz red sugarpaste
caster (superfine) sugar, to sprinkle
10 sugar hearts
sugar crystals

Method:
Preheat the oven to 190°C (165° fan), 375F, gas 5 and place 10 paper cases in a bun tin.

Beat the butter in a mixing bowl until soft and creamy. Beat in both sugars until smooth. Mix in the eggs, one at a time until smooth. Sift in the flour, baking powder and cocoa and fold in. Stir in the milk and chocolate chips.

Spoon the mixture into the paper cases and bake for 25 minutes until golden and firm to the touch. Leave in the tins for 5 minutes, then place on a wire rack to cool completely.

For the chocolate icing, melt the chocolate and butter in a heatproof bowl over a pan of simmering water. Sift in the icing sugar and water and beat until smooth. Quickly spread the topping over the cakes, as it will set quickly.

To decorate, roll out the sugar paste thinly on a surface dusted with caster sugar. Cut into heart shapes and arrange on the cakes. Place the sugar hearts on the cakes and sprinkle with sugar crystals.

Snowmen cupcakes

Prep and cook time: 50 minutes
makes: 12

Ingredients:
225 g | 8 oz | 1 cup butter
225 g | 8 oz | 1 cup caster
(superfine) sugar
4 eggs, beaten
225 g | 8 oz | 2 cups self-raising flour
110 g | 4 oz | 1 cup plain
(all-purpose) flour
60 g | 2 oz ground almonds
1 tbsp lemon juice
1 ½ tbsp milk

To decorate:
icing (confectioners') sugar
225 g | 8 oz ready-to-roll white
fondant icing
60 g | 2 oz apricot jam (jelly)
1 tbsp hot water
12 small white marshmallows
2 tubes coloured cake decorating
icing, red and black
edible silver baubles
red candy strawberry laces

Method:
For the cupcakes, heat the oven to 180°C (155° fan), 350F, gas 4 and place 12 paper cases in a bun tin.

Beat the butter and sugar in a mixing bowl until light and creamy. Gradually beat in half the egg. Sift a tablespoon of self-raising flour and beat well. Beat in the remaining egg and another tablespoon of self-raising flour.

Sift in both remaining flours and gently fold into the mixture with the almonds, lemon juice and milk. Spoon the mixture into the paper cases and bake for 20-25 minutes until risen and golden. Place on a wire rack to cool.

To decorate, dust a work surface with icing sugar and roll out the fondant icing to a 5 mm / ¼ " thickness. Cut out 12 circles using a small, smooth-edged pastry cutter, to fit the top of the cupcakes.

Mix the apricot jam with the hot water and brush over the surface of the cakes, to stick the circles of fondant on top. Attach the marshmallows for the snowmen's heads, with a little of the apricot jam.

Roll the remaining fondant icing into small balls for the noses. Brush lightly with apricot jam and stick to the marshmallow.

Pipe 2 small dots of black decorating icing for the eyes and red decorating icing for the mouths. Using a dab of apricot jam, stick on the edible silver baubles for buttons. Wrap the strawberry laces around the marshmallows for scarves.

Clementine cupcakes

Prep and cook time: 1 hour
makes: 24

Ingredients:
140 g | 5 oz butter, softened
140 g | 5 oz caster | ¾ cup caster
(superfine) sugar
100 g | 3 ½ oz 1 cup self-raising flour
25 g | 1 oz cornflour (cornstarch)
3 eggs

For the topping:
225 ml | 1 cup water
225 g | 8 oz | 1 cup sugar
6 clementines, thinly sliced
110 g | 4 oz | 1 cup pecan nuts, chopped

Method:
For the cupcakes, heat the oven to 190°C (165° fan), 375F, gas 5 and place 24 paper cases in a bun tin.

Put all the cake ingredients in a large bowl and beat until smooth. Spoon the mixture into the paper cases and bake for 12-15 minutes, until risen and golden. Cool on a wire rack.

For the topping, heat the water and sugar in a pan, stirring until the sugar is dissolved. Add the clementine slices and simmer gently, turning them over after 20 minutes. Gently simmer for 35 minutes, or until the peel on the slices starts to become translucent. Add the pecan nuts for the last 5 minutes.

Place a clementine slice on top of each cake and scatter with pecan nuts.

Hazelnut cinnamon cupcakes

Prep and cook time: 1 hour
makes: 12

Ingredients:
100 g | 3 ½ oz wholemeal flour
100 g | 3 ½ oz plain (all-purpose) flour
50 g | 2 oz finely ground
hazelnuts (cobnuts)
2 tbsp cocoa powder
1 tsp ground cinnamon
2 tsp baking powder
½ tsp bicarbonate of soda
(baking soda)
100 g | 3 ½ oz sugar
120 g | 4 ½ oz butter, melted
100 ml | ½ cup milk
2 eggs

To decorate:
1 tbsp cornflour (cornstarch)
2 tsp sugar
1 egg yolk
125 ml | 4 ½ fl. oz | ½ cup milk
1 tsp vanilla extract
75 g | 2 ½ oz unsalted butter
75 g | 2 ½ oz | ½ cup icing
(confectioners') sugar
2-3 tbsp edible silver baubles
12 small edible snowflakes

Method:

For the cupcakes, heat the oven to 180°C (160° fan) 350F, gas 4. Place 12 cupcake cases in a cupcake tin. Combine both flours with the nuts, cocoa, cinnamon, baking powder and bicarbonate of soda.

Beat the eggs lightly with the sugar and melted butter in a mixing bowl. Stir the cocoa-nut mixture into the egg mixture, stirring until smooth. Add enough milk to give a soft dropping consistency.

Spoon the mixture into the cases and bake for 25-30 minutes until risen and firm to the touch. Allow the cakes to cool on a wire rack.

To decorate, mix the cornflour with the sugar and egg yolk until smooth. Heat the milk in a pan until simmering. Pour the hot milk into the egg yolk mixture and stir until smooth. Return the mixture to the pan and heat, stirring all the time until the custard has thickened. Remove from the heat and leave to cool, stirring occasionally to prevent a skin forming.

Beat the butter until creamy. Sift in the icing sugar and beat well. Beat in the cool custard and the vanilla until smooth. Chill to firm the mixture.

Spoon the mixture into a piping bag and pipe onto the cooled cupcakes. Sprinkle with silver baubles and refrigerate until ready to serve. Top with the snowflakes.

Birthday cupcakes

Prep and cook time: 40 minutes
makes: 12

Ingredients:
120 g | 4 ½ oz soft butter
120 g | 4 ½ oz sugar
2 eggs
250 g | 9 oz | 2 ¼ cups plain
(all-purpose) flour
80 g | 3 oz dark (plain)
chocolate, chopped
1 tsp baking powder
½ tsp bicarbonate of soda
(baking soda)
a pinch of salt
225 ml | 7 ½ fl. oz | 1 cup natural
(plain) yoghurt

For the icing:
250 ml | 1 cup cream
1 tbsp icing (confectioners') sugar

To decorate:
2 tbsp white sugar sprinkles
2 tbsp red sugar sprinkles
12 small candles

Method:
For the cupcakes, heat the oven to 200°C (175° fan), 400F, gas 6 and place 12 large paper cases in a muffin tin.

Whisk the butter with the eggs and sugar until creamy.
Sift in the flour, salt, baking powder and bicarbonate of soda, until just combined. Gently stir in the yoghurt, followed by the chopped chocolate.

Spoon the mixture into the paper cases and bake for about 25 minutes until risen and golden. Cool in the tins for 10 minutes, then place on a wire rack to cool completely.

For the icing, whisk the cream until thick and firm and then stir in the icing sugar.

Spread the icing over the cakes and decorate with white and red sprinkles.

Frankenstein cupcakes

Prep and cook time: 50 minutes
makes: 12

Ingredients:
250 g | 9 oz | 2 ¼ cups plain
(all-purpose) flour
1 tbsp baking powder
75 g | 3 oz sugar
175 ml | 6 fl. oz | ¾ cup milk
1 egg, beaten
100 g | 3 ½ oz butter, melted
110 g | 4 oz | ⅓ cup orange
marmalade

For the icing:
140 g | 5 oz unsalted butter
250 g | 9 oz | 2 cups icing
(confectioners') sugar
1 tsp vanilla extract
orange food dye
blue food dye

To decorate:
12 white marshmallows
green food dye
blue food dye
12 green jelly candies, halved
12 red candies
1 tube decorating icing, brown

Method:
For the cupcakes, heat the oven to 200°C (180° fan) 400F, gas 6 and place 12 paper cases in a cupcake tin.

Sift the plain flour, baking powder and salt into a bowl and stir in the caster sugar. Beat the milk, egg, melted butter, orange zest and juice together. Add to the flour along with the marmalade.

Spoon the mixture equally into the paper cases and bake for 20-25 minutes until risen and golden brown. Cool on a wire rack.

For the icing, beat the butter in a bowl until light and creamy. Gradually sift in the icing sugar and beat well until smooth, then stir in the vanilla. Add a few drops of blue food dye to the icing, mixing thoroughly and then spread on top of the cakes.

To decorate, insert cocktail sticks in 12 marshmallows. Put a little water and green food dye in a small bowl and stir. Using a small brush, paint on the marshmallows, just enough to taint them and then let them dry.

Pipe hair, eyes, and mouths onto the green marshmallows for features. Remove the toothpicks and then place on top of the cupcakes, pushing the marshmallows down into the icing. Place 2 halves of green jelly candies and a red candy on the blue-topped cakes.

Easter cupcakes

Prep and cook time: 45 minutes
makes: 10

Ingredients:
225 g | 8 oz marzipan, finely chopped
75 g | 2 ½ oz unsalted butter
100 g | 3 ½ oz caster (superfine) sugar
3 eggs, beaten
1 tbsp milk
100 g | 3 ½ oz ground almonds
150 g | 5 oz | 1 ¼ cups plain
(all-purpose) flour
2 tsp baking powder
1 tsp almond extract

To decorate:
250 g | 9 oz | 1 ½ cups icing
(confectioners') sugar
2-3 tbsp hot water
225 g | 8 oz white marzipan
orange food dye
green food dye
3 tsp apricot jam (jelly)

Method:

For the cupcakes, heat the oven to 180°C (160° fan) 350F, gas 4. Place 10 paper cases in a cupcake tin.

Beat the marzipan, butter and sugar in a mixing bowl to a smooth paste. Whisk in the eggs gradually, until the mixture is smooth.

Gently fold in the almonds, flour and baking powder until well blended. Spoon the mixture into the paper cases and bake for 20-25 minutes until risen and springy to the touch. Place the cupcakes on a wire rack to cool.

For the icing, sift the icing sugar into a bowl and stir in enough hot water to give a thick coating consistency. Spoon the icing over the cakes

For the marzipan carrots, reserve ¼ of the marzipan for the leaves. Knead orange dye into the larger piece of marzipan until the colour is even.

Roll the dough into small balls and roll the balls between your palms, elongating them into thin tubes and tapering one end, so that they are shaped like carrots. Make horizontal indentations using a toothpick, along the length of the carrots to create slight creases.

Knead the green dye into the smaller piece of marzipan. Flatten small pieces and mark them into leaf shapes. Attach to the carrots with a dab of apricot jelly. Place the carrots on the cakes.

celebration.

Independence Day cupcakes

Prep and cook time: 55 minutes
makes: 12

Ingredients:
50 g | 2 oz | ¼ cup butter, melted
2 eggs, beaten
175 ml | 6 fl. oz | ¾ cup milk
225 g | 8 oz | 2 cups plain
(all-purpose) flour
4 tsp baking powder
2 tsp ground cinnamon
110 g | 4 oz | ½ cup caster
(superfine) sugar
a pinch of salt

To decorate:
2 egg whites
a pinch of salt
300 g | 10 oz caster (superfine) sugar
75 ml | 2 ½ fl. oz water
¼ tsp cream of tartar
1 tsp vanilla extract
red sugar stars
blue sugar stars
red sparkling sugar crystals
blue sparkling sugar crystals

Method:
Heat the oven to 200C° (180° fan) 400F, gas 6 and place paper cases in a 12 hole cupcake tin.

Mix together the butter, eggs and milk. Sift the flour, baking powder and cinnamon into a separate mixing bowl and then stir in the sugar.

Pour the egg mixture into the dry ingredients and stir until only just combined and the mixture is still slightly lumpy.

Spoon the mixture into the cupcake tins. Bake for 15-20 minutes until risen and golden. Leave the cupcakes in the tins for 5 minutes then place on a wire rack to cool completely.

For the icing, put all the ingredients except the vanilla into a heatproof bowl over a pan of simmering water. Whisk for 7-8 minutes until the icing thickens and forms firm peaks. Remove from the heat and add the vanilla. Beat until thick and spreadable.

To decorate, spoon the icing onto half the cupcakes and spread with a palette knife to form a smooth flat surface. Swirl the icing onto the other cupcakes into peaks. Decorate some cupcakes with sugar stars. Use a stencil to sprinkle the sugar crystals into stars and wavy lines on the remaining cupcakes.

Cinnamon Christmas cupcakes

Prep and cook time: 40 minutes
makes: 12

Ingredients:
80 g | 2 ½ oz | ⅔ cup dark
chocolate, grated
200 g | 7 oz | 1 ⅔ cups plain
(all-purpose) flour
50 g | 2 oz | ¼ cup sugar
50 ml | 2 fl. oz vegetable oil
50 ml | 2 fl. oz milk
2 tbsp cocoa powder
2 tsp ground ginger
2 tsp ground cinnamon
1 tbsp rum
2 eggs

To decorate:
200 g | 7 oz | ⅔ cup white
chocolate, chopped
75 ml | 2 ½ fl. oz | ⅓ cup cream
50 g | ¼ cup butter
15 g | ½ oz baking powder
50 g | ¼ cup marzipan
red food dye
green sugar strands

Method:
For the cupcakes, heat the oven to 200°C (180° fan) 400F,
gas 6 and place 12 paper cases in a cupcake tin.

Mix the chocolate with the flour, cocoa powder, ground
spices and the baking powder. Beat the eggs with the
sugar and oil. Quickly beat the flour mixture into the eggs,
adding the rum and as much milk as required to achieve
a dropping consistency.

Spoon the mixture into the paper cases and bake for
20-25 minutes. Test with a wooden toothpick, if it comes
out clean, the cupcakes are done.

To decorate, place the white chocolate in a bowl. Heat the
cream, let it cool slightly and pour over the chocolate, stirring
until the chocolate has melted. Add the butter and beat until
the mixture is glossy. Chill in the fridge until half set.

Knead the marzipan with a little icing sugar and the food dye,
until the marzipan is dark red. Roll out the marzipan paste on
a surface dusted with icing sugar to a 5 mm / ¼ " thickness
and cut out 12 small stars.

Spoon the semi-set chocolate cream into a piping bag and
top the cooled cupcakes with swirls of chocolate cream.
Decorate with the marzipan stars and green sugar strands.

Nougat Christmas cupcakes

Prep and cook time: 35 minutes
makes: 12

Ingredients:
110 g | 4 oz | ½ cup butter, softened
110 g | 4 oz | ½ cup sugar
2 eggs
110 g | 4 oz | 1 cup self-raising flour
1 tsp baking powder
25 g | 1 oz cocoa powder
1 tsp mixed spice

To decorate:
300 ml | 10 fl. oz | 1 ⅓ cups cream
30 g | 1 oz icing (confectioners') sugar
1 tsp vanilla extract
110 g | 4 oz chocolate coated almond
nougat, roughly chopped

Method:
Preheat the oven to 170°C (150° fan) 325F, gas 3 and place 12 paper cases in a cupcake tin.

Put all the cake ingredients into a mixing bowl and beat until combined.

Spoon the mixture into the paper cases and bake for 15-20 minutes until risen and firm. Cool the cupcakes on a wire rack.

For the Chantilly cream, whisk the cream until thick, then sift in the icing sugar. Add the vanilla. Whisk for a few minutes until thick enough to pipe.

Spoon the cream into a piping bag and pipe on top of the cakes. Scatter chopped nougat over the cream.

Chocolate Christmas cupcakes

Prep and cook time: 50 minutes
makes: 12

Ingredients:
150 g | 5 oz | ½ cup honey
100 g | 3 ½ oz | ½ cup dark brown sugar
75 g | 3 oz butter
3 tbsp milk
250 g | 9 oz | 2 ½ cups plain (all-purpose) flour
2 tsp baking powder
1 pinch ground cardamom
¼ tsp ground cloves
2 tsp ground cinnamon
1 tsp mixed spice
2 tbsp cocoa powder
2 eggs
100 g | 3 ½ oz | ½ cup almonds, chopped

To decorate:
2 egg whites
2 tsp lemon juice
330 g | 11 ½ oz | 3 cups icing (confectioners') sugar, sifted
200 g | 7 oz marzipan
red food dye
green food dye

Method:
For the cupcakes, heat the oven to 170°C (150°fan) 325F, gas 3. Place 12 paper cases in a cupcake tin.

Warm the honey, sugar, butter and milk in a pan over a low heat until the sugar dissolves and allow it to cool.

Sift the flour, baking powder, spices and cocoa together and stir into the cooled honey mixture. Stir in the eggs and fold in the chopped almonds.

Spoon the mixture into the paper cases and bake for 25 minutes. Leave in the tins for 5 minutes then cool on a wire rack.

With an electric mixer or whisk, beat the egg whites with the lemon juice until combined. Add the sifted icing sugar and beat on a low speed until combined and smooth. The icing needs to be used immediately or transferred to an airtight container as it hardens when exposed to air.

To decorate, take 50 g of the marzipan and knead in a few drops of red food dye. Roll into tiny balls for the berries.

Knead green food dye into the remaining marzipan. Roll the green marzipan out thinly on a surface dusted with icing sugar. Cut out 24 holly leaves and mark the veins with a cocktail stick. Decorate the cupcakes with leaves and berries.

Valentine's Day cupcakes

Prep and cook time: 50 minutes
makes: 12

Ingredients:
50 g | 2 oz dark (plain) chocolate
110 g | 4 oz | ½ cup butter
100 g | 3 ½ oz plain (all-purpose) flour
1 tsp bicarbonate of soda
(baking soda)
1 tbsp cocoa powder
200 g | 7 oz light brown sugar
1 egg, beaten
75 g | 2 ½ oz | ½ cup chocolate chips
125 ml | 4 fl. oz | ½ cup hot water

For the chocolate ganache:
250 ml | 1 cup cream
250 g | 10 oz dark (plain) chocolate

Method:
Preheat the oven to 180°C (160° fan) 350F, gas 4 and place 12 paper cases in a cupcake tin.

Melt the chocolate and butter in a heatproof bowl over a pan of simmering water. Remove from the heat and stir once, then set aside to cool.

Sift the flour, bicarbonate of soda and cocoa powder into a mixing bowl and stir in the sugar.

Slowly stir the egg into the melted chocolate. Stir the egg mixture into the dry ingredients with the chocolate chips. Stir in the hot water, until only just combined.

Spoon the mixture into the paper cases and bake for 25-30 minutes until risen and firm. Cool in the tins for 10 minutes, then place the cupcakes on a wire rack to cool completely.

For the chocolate ganache, heat the cream in a pan and bring to a boil. Immediately remove from the heat and pour over the chocolate and stir until the chocolate has melted. Chill until the mixture is thick enough to pipe.

Put the ganache into a piping bag and pipe on top of the cakes. Decorate with ribbons and paper roses.

Easter egg cupcakes

Prep and cook time: 45 minutes
makes: 20

Ingredients:
150 g | 5 oz butter
150 g | 5 oz sugar
1 tsp vanilla extract
3 eggs
200 g | 7 oz | 1 ¾ cups self-raising flour
½ tsp baking powder
1 pinch salt

To decorate:
600 ml | 20 fl. oz | 2 ½ cups cream
4 tbsp icing (confectioners') sugar
1 tsp vanilla extract
20 small chocolate Easter eggs

Method:
Preheat the oven to 180°C (160° fan) 350F, gas 4 and place 20 paper cases in cupcake tins.

Beat the butter with the sugar and vanilla until soft and light. Beat in the eggs, eggs one by one. Sift in the flour, baking powder and salt and mix well until smooth.

Spoon the mixture into the paper cases and bake for 20-30 minutes until golden and springy to the touch. Leave the cupcakes in the tins for 5 minutes, then place on a wire rack to cool completely.

For the icing, whisk the cream until thickened, sift in the icing sugar and whisk until thick. Stir in the vanilla.

Spoon the icing into a piping bag and pipe a whirl on top of each cake. Decorate with chocolate eggs.

Star spangled cupcakes

Prep and cook time: 40 minutes
makes: 14

Ingredients:
25 g | 1 oz cocoa powder
100 ml | 3 ½ fl. oz boiling water
50 g | 2 oz | ¼ cup butter
100 g | 3 ½ oz caster (superfine) sugar
1 egg, beaten
85 g | 3 ½ oz plain (all-purpose) flour
½ tsp bicarbonate of soda
(baking soda)
¼ tsp baking powder

For the topping:
175 g | 6 oz | ¾ cup unsalted butter
350 g | 12 oz | 2 ¼ cups icing
(confectioners') sugar
2 tsp lemon juice
6 tsp hot water

To decorate:
red, white and blue sugar stars

Method:
Preheat the oven to 180°C (155° fan), 350F, gas 4 and place 14 medium paper cases in a muffin tin.

Put the cocoa and boiling water into a small bowl and mix to a smooth paste and allow it to cool. Beat the butter and sugar in a mixing bowl until soft and light, then beat in the egg.

Sift in the dry ingredients and stir until blended. Stir in the cocoa paste and mix until smooth.

Spoon the mixture into the paper cases and bake for 20 minutes until risen and springy to the touch. Remove from the tins and cool on a wire rack.

For the icing, beat the butter until soft. Sift in the icing sugar and stir well. Beat in the lemon juice and hot water until the mixture is smooth.

Spoon the mixture into a piping bag and pipe swirls on top of the cooled cakes. Scatter the sugar stars over the top.

Halloween cupcakes

Prep and cook time: 45 minutes
makes: 12

Ingredients:
175 g | 6 oz | ¾ cup butter
175 g | 6 oz | 1 cup light brown sugar
3 eggs, beaten
25 ml | 1 fl. oz black
treacle (molasses)
225 g | 8 oz | 2 cups self-raising flour
2 tsp ground ginger
2 tbsp ground almonds
30 ml | 1 fl. oz | ⅛ cup cream

For the icing:
150 g | 5 oz unsalted butter
350 g | 2 ¼ cups icing
(confectioners') sugar
few drops vanilla extract

To decorate:
red piping icing
brown piping icing
mini marshmallows
chocolate candies
chocolate twig candies (Matchmakers),
cut into pieces
thin strips of ready rolled fondant icing
12 blue chocolate-coated candies

Method:

For the cupcakes, heat the oven to 180°C (155° fan), 350F, gas 4 and place 12 paper cases in a bun tin.

Beat the butter and sugar in a mixing bowl until soft. Gradually beat in the eggs and then stir in the treacle. Sift in the flour and ginger and fold in gently. Stir in the ground almonds and cream until blended and smooth.

Spoon the mixture into the paper cases and bake for 20 minutes until springy to the touch. Cool in the tins for 5 minutes, then place on a wire rack to cool completely.

For the icing, beat the butter until very soft. Sift in the icing sugar and beat until smooth. Divide the icing in half and add food dye to 1 bowl.

Frankenstein cupcakes:

Spread the green icing on top of the cakes. Decorate with chocolate candies for the eyes, pipe red piping icing for the mouth and pipe 2 dots of brown piping icing for the noses. Place a few chocolate candies above the eyes and press in the chocolate twig candies for the hair. Attach mini marshmallows with cocktail sticks into the side of the cupcake, to look like neck bolts.

Mummy cupcakes:

Spread the plain icing over the remaining cupcakes, and then lay thin strips of fondant icing over the top. Place 2 blue candies per cupcake, as eyes, half underneath one strip of fondant icing.

Reindeer cupcakes

Prep and cook time: 50 minutes
makes: 12

Ingredients:
110 g | 4 oz | ½ cup butter
110 g | 4 oz | ½ cup sugar
2 eggs, beaten
1 clementine, zest
110 g | 4 oz | 1 cup self-raising flour
½ tsp baking powder
1 tsp vanilla extract

To decorate:
175 g | 6 oz | 1 ¼ cups icing
(confectioners') sugar
30 ml | 1 fl. oz lemon juice
1 tsp hot water
450 g | 1 lb brown sugarpaste
225 g | 8 oz cream sugarpaste
1 tube decorating icing, red
1 tube decorating icing, black

Method:

For the cupcakes, heat the oven to 180°C (160° fan) 350F, gas 4. Place 12 paper cases in a cupcake tin.

Cream the butter and sugar in a mixing bowl until light and creamy. Add the eggs gradually, beating well and stir in the clementine zest. Sift in the flour and baking powder and gently fold into the mixture, then stir in the vanilla.

Spoon the mixture into the paper cases and bake for 12-15 minutes until springy to the touch.

For the icing, sift the icing sugar into a bowl and gradually stir in the lemon juice and water until smooth and thick. Spoon a little icing onto each cooled cupcake and smooth level with a palette knife.

To decorate, roll pieces of the brown sugarpaste into 24 thick, slightly flattened oval shapes to form the 2 sections of the reindeers' faces. Dampen with a little water and attach to the icing. Shape the ears from sugarpaste and mark the centres with a cocktail stick or sharp knife. Attach to the faces.

Roll out the cream sugarpaste on a surface lightly dusted with icing sugar. Shape 12 pieces for the antlers and mark with a cocktail stick. Attach to the faces with a little water.

Use the decorating icing to pipe eyes, a nose and a mouth onto the reindeer.

Spider cupcakes

Prep and cook time: 45 minutes
makes: 12

Ingredients:
75 g | 2 ½ oz butter, softened
200 g | 7 oz sugar
a pinch of salt
1 tsp vanilla extract
1 egg
100 ml | 3 ½ fl. oz milk
1 tsp vinegar
300 g | 10 ½ oz | 2 ½ cups plain
(all-purpose) flour
2 tsp baking powder
75 g | 2 ½ oz cocoa powder
80 g | 2 ½ oz dark (plain)
chocolate, grated

To decorate:
4-5 tbsp apricot jam (jelly), warmed
40 liquorice strips, halved
12 mini mallomar cookies (or small
chocolate marshmallow biscuits)
12 pieces black and white liquorice
candy, halved
24 orange sugar pearls

Method:

For the cupcakes, heat the oven to 170°C (150° fan) 325F, gas 3. Place 12 paper cases in a cupcake tin.

Beat the butter with the sugar, salt and vanilla in a mixing bowl until creamy. Beat in the egg followed by the milk and vinegar.

Sift in the flour, baking powder and cocoa and stir into the butter mixture until blended, then stir in the grated chocolate.

Spoon the mixture into the paper cases and bake for about 20 minutes until springy to the touch. Leave the cakes to cool in the tins for 5 minutes then place on a wire rack to cool completely.

To decorate, brush the centre of the cakes with a little apricot jam and attach the cookies for the body. Attach the liquorice strips for the legs with a little apricot jam, then add the liquorice candies and sugar pearls for the eyes using a little apricot jam.

Vanilla cupcakes

Prep and cook time: 40 minutes
makes: 10

Ingredients:
175 g | 6 oz | ¾ cup butter
175 g | 6 oz | ¾ cup caster
(superfine) sugar
4 eggs, beaten
1 tsp vanilla extract
175 g | 6 oz | 1 ½ cups self-raising flour

For the vanilla buttercream:
75 g | 3 oz butter
175 g | 6 oz | 1 ¼ cups icing
(confectioners') sugar
½ tsp vanilla extract

Method:
For the cupcakes, heat the oven to 180°C (155° fan), 350F, gas 4 and place 10 medium paper cases in a bun tin.

Beat the butter and sugar in a mixing bowl until soft and creamy. Beat in the eggs, a little at a time, until smooth. Gently stir in the vanilla and flour.

Spoon the mixture into the paper cases and bake for 20 minutes until golden and springy to the touch. Remove from the tin and cool on a wire rack.

For the vanilla buttercream, beat the butter until soft. Sift in the icing sugar and beat well until smooth. Stir in the vanilla.

Spread the buttercream over the top of the cakes. Sift icing sugar over the top of each cake.

Skeleton cupcakes

Prep and cook time: 35 minutes
makes: 10

Ingredients:
175 g | 6 oz | ¾ cup butter
175 g | 6 oz | ¾ cup caster
(superfine) sugar
4 eggs, beaten
1 orange, finely grated zest
1 tsp vanilla extract
175 g | 6 oz | 1 ½ cups self-raising flour

For the chocolate icing:
110 g | 4 oz dark (plain) chocolate
2 tbsp butter
125 ml | 4 fl. oz | ½ cup crème fraiche
50 g | 2 oz icing (confectioners')
sugar, sifted

To decorate:
10 white mini marshmallows
80 liquorice comfits (torpedoes)
brown piping icing

Method:
For the cupcakes, heat the oven to 180°C (155° fan), 350F, gas 4 and place 10 paper cases in a bun tin.

Beat the butter and sugar in a mixing bowl until soft and light. Beat in the eggs, a little at time until well blended. Gently stir in the orange zest, vanilla and flour.

Spoon the mixture into the paper cases and bake for 20 minutes until golden and springy to the touch. Remove from the tin and cool on a wire rack.

For the chocolate icing, melt the chocolate and butter in a heatproof bowl over a pan of simmering water. Remove from the heat and allow it to cool slightly. Stir in the crème fraiche until blended, then stir in the icing sugar. Spread the icing over the top of each cake.

To decorate, place a mini marshmallow on each cake for the head and pipe the mouth and eyes with brown piping icing. Attach the liquorice comfits to each cake to form the body, arms and legs.

153

Candy heart cupcakes

Prep and cook time: 35 minutes
makes: 12

Ingredients:
100 g | 3 ½ oz dark (plain)
chocolate, chopped
200 g | 7 oz | 1 ¾ cups self-raising flour
225 g | 8 oz light brown sugar
90 g | 3 oz cocoa powder
150 ml | 5 fl. oz | ⅔ cup sunflower oil
100 ml | 3 ½ fl. oz soured cream
2 eggs
1 tsp vanilla extract
100 ml | 3 ½ fl. oz warm water

For the icing:
150 g | 5 oz unsalted butter
350 g | 12 oz | 2 ¼ cups icing
(confectioners') sugar
few drops vanilla extract
25 g | 1 oz dark (plain)
chocolate, melted
2 tsp lemon juice
yellow food dye
candy hearts

Method:

For the cupcakes, heat the oven to 180°C (155° fan), 350F, gas 4 and place 12 paper cases in a bun tin.

Melt the chocolate in a heatproof bowl over a pan of simmering water. Whisk the flour, sugar, cocoa, oil, soured cream, eggs, vanilla and water until smooth. Whisk in the melted chocolate.

Spoon into the paper cases and bake for 20 minutes. To test if they're cooked, insert a wooden tooth pick, if it comes out clean, the cakes are done. Remove from the tins and cool on a wire rack.

For the icing, beat the butter until very soft. Sift in the icing sugar and beat until smooth. Divide the buttercream into 3 and put 2 portions into 2 small bowls.

Stir the vanilla extract into ⅓ of the mixture, the melted chocolate into ⅓ and the lemon juice and yellow dye into the remaining ⅓. Spread the buttercream over the top of each cake and decorate with candy hearts.

154

Mince pie cupcakes

Prep and cook time: 35 minutes
makes: 12

Ingredients:
2 eggs
110 g | 4 oz | ½ cup caster (superfine) sugar
50 ml | 2 fl. oz cream
110 g | 4 oz | ½ cup mincemeat
110 g | 4 oz | 1 cup self-raising flour
½ tsp baking powder
1 tsp ground cinnamon
½ tsp nutmeg, freshly grated
2 tsp sherry
20 g | 1 oz butter, melted

To decorate:
110 g | 4 oz white marzipan
red food dye
green food dye
icing (confectioners') sugar

Method:
For the cupcakes, heat the oven to 180°C (160° fan), 350F, gas 4, and place paper cases in a 12 hole bun tin.

Mix the eggs and sugar together and beat in the cream. Gently stir in the mincemeat.

Sift in the flour, baking powder and spices and fold in until incorporated. Stir in the sherry and butter until well mixed.

Spoon the mixture into the paper cases and bake for 12-15 minutes until risen and springy to the touch. Cool on a wire rack.

For the decoration, divide the marzipan in half. Knead a few drops of red dye into one half and green into the other half.

Roll out the marzipan on a surface lightly dusted with icing sugar. Cut out stars with a small star-shaped cookie cutter.

Place the marzipan decorations on top of each cake and sift over a layer of icing sugar.

Pumpkin cupcakes

Prep and cook time: 50 minutes
makes: 10

Ingredients:
195 g | 7 oz | 1 ½ cups plain
(all-purpose) flour
1 tsp bicarbonate of soda
(baking soda)
1 tsp ground cinnamon
¼ tsp ground ginger
¼ tsp ground cloves
½ teaspoon salt
110 g | 4 oz | ½ cup unsalted butter
200 g | 7 oz | 1 cup white sugar
2 large eggs
1 tsp vanilla extract
75 g | 2 ½ oz | ¾ cup canned pumpkin
puree, or boiled, pureed pumpkin

To decorate:
250 g | 9 oz | 1 ½ cups icing
(confectioners') sugar
1 egg white
orange food dye
yellow food dye
2-3 tbsp orange sparkling
sugar crystals
caster (superfine) sugar
110 g | 4 oz green sugar paste
5 chocolate covered candies

Method:
For the cupcakes, heat the oven to 180°C (160° fan) 350F, gas 4. Place paper cases in 10 holes of a muffin tin. In a large bowl, sift together the flour, bicarbonate of soda, ground spices and salt.

Cream the butter and sugar until light and fluffy. Add the eggs, one at a time, beating well. Beat in the vanilla extract. Alternately add the flour mixture and pumpkin puree, stirring each time.

Fill the paper cases evenly with the batter. Place in the oven and bake for about 18 - 20 minutes, or until firm and golden. Place the cupcakes on a wire rack to cool.

For the icing, sift the icing sugar into a bowl. Lightly beat the egg white and mix with the icing sugar. Put ¼ of the mixture into another bowl and tint with yellow food dye. Add orange food dye to the remaining ¾ of the icing. Whisk well for 3-4 minutes until stiff. Cover the yellow icing bowl with a damp cloth to prevent drying out.

Spread the orange icing over the cupcakes and sprinkle with the orange sugar crystals and leave to set. Put the yellow icing into a piping bag, you may need to thin it with a little water to achieve a piping consistency. Pipe lines on top of the orange icing to resemble a pumpkin.

Roll out the green sugar paste thinly on a surface dusted with caster sugar. Cut out leaves. Attach the leaves to the cakes with a dab of piping icing. Attach the chocolate candies in the centre of each cake as stalks.

Gingerbread cupcakes

Prep and cook time: 45 minutes
makes: 12

Ingredients:
250 g | 9 oz | 2 ½ cups plain
(all-purpose) flour
225 g | 8 oz | 1 ¼ cups light
brown sugar
2 tsp baking powder
2 tsp ground ginger
½ teaspoon ground cinnamon
a pinch of ground cloves
2 eggs
100 ml | 3 ½ fl. oz clear honey
110 g | 4 oz | ½ cup butter, melted
175 ml | 6 fl. oz | ¾ cup hot water
2 tbsp chopped stem ginger

To decorate:
50 ml | 2 fl. oz syrup, from a jar
of preserved ginger
6 glace (candied) cherries, halved
60 blanched almonds, whole
edible gold and silver baubles

Method:
Heat the oven to 180°C (160° fan) 350F, gas 4. Place 12 paper cases in a cupcake tin.

Sift the flour, sugar, baking powder and spices into a mixing bowl. Beat together the eggs, honey and butter until smooth. Stir into the dry ingredients. Add the water and chopped ginger and stir well until combined.

Spoon the mixture into the paper cases and bake for 20-25 minutes until golden. Leave in the tins for 10 minutes then place on a wire rack to cool.

To decorate, brush the top of the cupcakes with ginger syrup. Place half a glace cherry in the centre of each cupcake and decorate with the almonds and baubles.

Carrot cupcakes

Prep and cook time: 45 minutes
makes: 18

Ingredients:
6 eggs, separated
250 g | 9 oz | 1 ¼ cups sugar
1 pinch salt
1 lemon, zest
300 g | 10 ½ oz | 2 cups
ground almonds
100 g | 3 ½ oz plain (all-purpose) flour
250 g | 9 oz carrots, grated

For the icing:
500 g | 17 ½ oz | 2 cups cream
cheese (soft)
50 g | 2 oz | ½ cup icing
(confectioners') sugar
30 ml | 1 fl. oz lemon juice

To decorate:
500 g | 1 lb strawberries, halved

Method:
For the cupcakes, heat the oven to 180°C (155° fan) 350F, gas 4 and place 18 cupcake cases in a bun tin.

Beat the egg yolks with the salt, lemon zest and ⅓ of the sugar, until fluffy. In a clean bowl, whisk the egg whites until they are firm and peaking. Gradually add the remaining sugar while whisking all the time and continue to whisk until the mixture is stiff, but not dry.

Stir in the ground almonds with the flour and grated carrots. Gently fold in ⅓ of the egg whites until incorporated. Gradually fold in the remaining egg whites until the mixture is smoothly blended.

Spoon the mixture into the cupcake cases and bake for 25-30 minutes, until the cakes feel firm to the touch. Remove from the tins and cool on a wire rack.

For the icing, beat the cream cheese with the sugar and lemon juice until smooth. Spread on the cupcakes and decorate with strawberries.

children's.

Sports ball cupcakes

Prep and cook time: 30 minutes
makes: 12

Ingredients:
110 g | 4 oz | ½ cup unsalted butter
110 g | 4 oz | ½ cup caster
(superfine) sugar
½ tsp vanilla extract
2 eggs, beaten
110 g | 4 oz | 1 cup self-raising flour

For the icing:
175 g | 6 oz | 1 cup icing
(confectioners') sugar
1 tbsp lemon juice
4-6 tsp water

For the buttercream:
50 g | 2 oz | ¼ cup unsalted butter
110 g | 4 oz | ¾ cup icing
(confectioners') sugar
½ orange, juice and zest
orange food dye

Method:

For the cupcakes, heat the oven to 180°C (155° fan), 350F, gas 4 and place 12 paper cases in a bun tin.

Cream the butter and the sugar together until light and fluffy. Add the vanilla, followed by the eggs. Slowly fold in the flour until combined and spoon the mixture into the paper cases.

Bake for approximately 10-12 minutes until risen and bouncy to the touch. Remove the cakes from the tin and cool on a wire rack.

For the icing, sift the icing sugar into a bowl and gradually mix in the lemon juice until smooth. Add just enough water to give a coating consistency.

For the buttercream, beat the butter until soft and creamy. Sift in the icing sugar and beat well. Gradually beat in enough orange juice to give a soft spreading consistency. Stir in the zest and a few drops of orange dye.

Decorating suggestions:

Spread the icing over 9 of the cakes. Cover 3 with yellow sugar strands. Add a swirl of white icing to create tennis ball cupcakes. Press 6 chocolate buttons each into 3 iced cakes. Decorate with brown piping gel when the icing has set to make football cupcakes. Cover 3 cakes with white sugar pearls and decorate with red piping gel for baseball cupcakes. Spread the orange butter cream over the remaining cakes and decorate with brown piping gel for basketball cupcakes.

50¢

Cupcakes with candy-coated chocolate

Prep and cook time: 40 minutes
makes: 12

Ingredients:
1 egg
75 ml | 2 ½ fl. oz | ⅓ cup sunflower oil
100 ml | 3 ½ fl. oz soured cream
200 g | 7 oz | 1 ¾ cups plain (all-purpose) flour
110 g | 4 oz | ½ cup sugar
2 tsp baking powder
a pinch of salt

To decorate:
150 g | 5 oz | 1 cup icing (confectioners') sugar
1 tbsp lemon juice
150 g | 5 oz candy-coated chocolate sweets

Method:
Preheat the oven to 200°C (180° fan) 400F, gas 6. Place 12 paper cases in a cupcake tin.

Mix the egg and oil, then stir in the soured cream. Combine the flour, sugar, baking powder and salt in a mixing bowl. Gently stir in the egg-oil mixture until only just combined. The mixture will be lumpy.

Spoon the mixture into the paper cases and bake for about 20 minutes until golden and firm to the touch. Cool the cupcakes on a wire rack.

For the icing, sift the icing sugar into a bowl and gradually beat in the lemon juice to make a thin icing. If it is too thick add a little water.

Spoon the icing on the cakes and decorate with chocolate sweets before the icing sets.

Vanilla chocolate cupcakes

Prep and cook time: 35 minutes
makes: 12

Ingredients:
175 g | 6 oz | 1 ¼ cups self-raising flour
a pinch of salt
110 g | 4 oz | ½ cup butter, softened
110 g | 4 oz | ½ cup caster
(superfine) sugar
2 eggs
1 tsp vanilla extract

To decorate:
175 g | 6 oz milk chocolate
110 g | 4 oz | ½ cup unsalted butter
1 tsp vanilla extract
white and brown sugar sprinkles

Method:
For the cupcakes, heat the oven to 190°C (165° fan), 375F, gas 5 and place 12 paper cases in a bun tin.

Put all the cupcake ingredients into a mixing bowl and beat until very smooth. Spoon the mixture into the paper cases and bake for 15-20 minutes until risen and golden. Remove the cakes from the tin and place on a wire rack to cool completely.

For the icing, melt the chocolate and butter in a pan over a very low heat. Remove from the heat, stir in the vanilla extract and leave to cool and thicken. Spread, or pipe the icing thickly over the top of the cakes and decorate with sprinkles.

Monster cupcakes

Prep and cook time: 35 minutes
makes: 12

Ingredients:
110 g | 4 oz | ½ cup butter
110 g | 4 oz | ½ cup sugar
2 eggs, beaten
75 g | 2 ½ oz | ¾ cup self-raising flour
25 g | 1 oz cocoa powder

To decorate:
125 g | 4 ½ oz green sugar paste
caster (superfine) sugar
250 ml | 8 ½ fl. oz | 1 cup cream
24 red jelly candies
12 pieces liquorice candy
110 g | 4 oz | ½ cup chocolate, grated

Method:
For the cupcakes, heat the oven to 190°C (165° fan) 375F, gas 5. Place paper cases in a 12 hole bun tin.

Cream the butter and sugar until light and fluffy. Gradually beat in the eggs and then sift in the flour and cocoa and gently fold into the mixture.

Spoon the mixture into the paper cases and bake for 15 minutes until risen and firm to the touch. Remove from the tin and place on a wire rack to cool.

To decorate, roll out the sugar paste thinly on a surface dusted with caster sugar and cut it into 6 long, thin strips. Cut each strip in half.

Whisk the cream until thick and spread on top of the cooled cupcakes. Place 2 red candies as eyes, a liquorice candy as a nose, a sugar paste strip as hair and grated chocolate as a mouth.

Fairy cakes

Prep and cook time: 45 minutes
makes: 12

Ingredients:
2 eggs
110 g | 4 oz | 1 cup self-raising flour
½ tsp baking powder
110 g | 4 oz | ½ cup butter, softened
110 g | 4 oz | ½ cup sugar
1 lemon, grated zest

To decorate:
250 g | 9 oz | 2 cups icing
(confectioners') sugar
3-4 tbsp lemon juice
1 tsp hot water
purple food dye
coloured sugar sprinkles
sugar numbers

Method:
Heat the oven to 170°C (150° fan) 325F, gas 3. Place 12 paper cases in a cupcake tin.

Put all the cake ingredients into a mixing bowl and whisk together until well combined.

Spoon the mixture into the paper cases and bake for 20-25 minutes until golden and springy to the touch. Remove the cakes from the tin and place on a wire rack to cool.

For the icing, sift the icing sugar into a bowl and gradually stir in the lemon juice and water until smooth and thick.

Put a little of the icing into 2 small bowls and stir a few drops of food dye into a bowl. Use the other small bowl of icing for drizzling over the iced cakes. Spread the icing over the cakes.

To decorate, drizzle contrasting icing over some cakes, add dots of icing to others and place a sugar number on top. Decorate the remaining cakes with sugar sprinkles.

Chocolate cupcakes

Prep and cook time: 30 minutes
makes: 10

Ingredients:
2 eggs
110 g | 4 oz | ½ cup caster
(superfine) sugar
50 ml | 2 oz cream
110 g | 4 oz | 1 cup self-raising flour
½ tsp baking powder
50 g | 2 oz | ¼ cup butter, melted

For the icing:
225 g | 8 oz | 1 ¾ cups icing
(confectioners') sugar
25 g | 1 oz cocoa powder
25 g | 1 oz sugar
45 ml | 1 ½ fl. oz water

To decorate:
coloured sugar sprinkles

Method:
For the cupcakes, heat the oven to 180°C (155° fan) 350F, gas 4 and place 10 paper cases in a bun tin.

Whisk the eggs and sugar together until light and then whisk in the cream. Sift in the flour and baking powder and fold in. Gently stir in the butter until blended.

Spoon the mixture into the paper cases and bake for 12-15 minutes until risen and golden and springy to the touch. Remove from the oven and leave to cool in the tins for 5 minutes. Place on a wire rack to cool completely.

For the icing, sift the icing sugar into a bowl, heat the cocoa, sugar and water in a pan over a low heat until the sugar has dissolved. Increase the heat to boiling point and remove from the heat. Pour onto the icing sugar and beat until smooth. Ice the cakes while warm as this icing sets quickly and scatter with sugar sprinkles.

Caterpillar cupcakes

Prep and cook time: 35 minutes
makes: 12

Ingredients:
110 g | 4 oz | ½ cup butter, softened
110 g | 4 oz | ½ cup caster
(superfine) sugar
110 g | 4 oz | 1 cup self-raising flour
½ tsp baking powder
1 tsp lemon juice
2 eggs, beaten

To decorate:
175 g | 6 oz | 1 ¼ cups icing
(confectioners') sugar
5-6 tsp hot water
green food dye
175 g | 6 oz white sugarpaste
chocolate buttons
orange sprinkles
thin strips black liquorice
2 strawberry laces, cut into small pieces

Method:
For the cupcakes, heat the oven to 180°C (155° fan), 350F, gas 4 and place paper cases in a 12 hole bun tin.

Beat the butter and sugar in a mixing bowl until light and fluffy. Add the eggs a little at a time until the mixture is smooth. Sift in the flour and baking powder and gently fold in. Stir in the lemon juice.

Spoon the mixture into the paper cases and bake for 13-15 minutes until golden and springy to the touch. Remove the cakes from the tin and cool on a wire rack.

For the icing, sift the icing sugar into a bowl and mix with the hot water until smooth. Add a few drops of green food dye and spread over the top of the cakes. Stick an orange candy in the centre of each cake for the nose.

Roll small amounts of sugarpaste into balls and stick on top of the icing for the eyes, Attach chocolate buttons to the sugarpaste balls with a small dab of icing. Attach 2 liquorice strips above the eyes for the feelers.

Sprinkle orange sprinkles on top of some of the cakes and attach liquorice strips to form legs. Place a small piece of strawberry lace on each cupcake for the mouth.

Pink-iced chocolate cupcakes

Prep and cook time: 40 minutes
makes: 12

Ingredients:
110 g | 4 oz | ½ cup butter, softened
110 g | 4 oz | ¾ cup dark brown sugar
75 g | 2 ½ | ¾ cup self-raising flour
25 g | 1 oz cocoa powder, sifted
a pinch of baking powder
2 eggs
1 tsp vanilla extract

To decorate:
300 ml | 10 fl. oz | 1 ⅓ cups cream
2 tbsp icing (confectioners') sugar
1 tbsp raspberry syrup
pink food dye
36 fruit candies
sugar sprinkles

Method:
For the cupcakes, heat the oven to 190°C (170° fan) 375F, gas 5 and place 12 cupcake cases in a bun tin.

Whisk together all the cake ingredients until smooth and blended. Spoon the mixture into the cupcake cases and bake for 15 minutes until well risen and firm to the touch. Place the cupcakes on a wire rack and leave to cool.

For the cream topping, whisk the cream until thick. Sift in the icing sugar and syrup and whisk until smooth and thick. Stir in a few drops of food dye.

Spoon the cream into a piping bag and pipe a swirl on each cake. Place 3 fruit candies in each swirl of cream and sprinkle with sugar sprinkles.

Noughts and crosses cupcakes

Prep and cook time: 30 minutes
makes: 12

Ingredients:
2 eggs
110 g | 4 oz | ½ cup caster
(superfine) sugar
50 ml | 2 fl. oz cream
1 small lemon, grated zest
1 small orange, grated zest
110 g | 4 oz | 1 cup self-raising flour
½ tsp baking powder
50 g | 2 oz | ¼ cup butter, melted

To decorate:
140 g | 5 oz unsalted butter
350 g | 12 oz | 2 ½ cups icing
(confectioners') sugar, sifted
140 g | 5 oz crème fraiche
½ tsp vanilla extract
blue food dye
candy-coated chocolate sweets

Method:
For the cupcakes, heat the oven to 180°C (155° fan) 350F, gas 4, and place paper cases in a 12 hole bun tin.

Whisk the eggs and sugar together until smooth, the beat in the cream and lemon and orange zests.

Sift in the flour and baking powder and fold into the mixture gently. Gently stir in the melted butter.

Spoon the mixture into the paper cases and bake for about 15 minutes until golden and springy to the touch. Leave the cupcakes to cool for 5 minutes then remove from the tin and cool completely on a wire rack.

To decorate, beat the butter until soft and creamy. Gradually whisk in the icing sugar and crème fraiche until smooth. Then add the vanilla and combine well. Place half of the mixture in another bowl and add a few drops of blue food dye.

Spread the buttercream over the top of the cakes and decorate with chocolate sweets.

Ice-cream cupcakes

Prep and cook time: 35 minutes
makes: 10

Ingredients:
140 g | 5 oz unsalted butter
140 g | 5 oz caster (superfine) sugar
75 g | 2 ½ oz | ½ cup polenta
(fine cornmeal)
3 eggs, beaten
140 g | 5 oz | 1 ¼ cups plain
(all-purpose) flour
1 tsp baking powder
1 tbsp milk
110 g | 4 oz | ½ cup glace
(candied) cherries, chopped

To decorate:
12 scoops vanilla ice cream, softened
12 candied cherries
pink sugar sprinkles

Method:
For the cupcakes, heat the oven to 180°C (160° fan) 350F, gas 4. Place 10 paper cases in a cupcake tin.

Beat together the butter and sugar in a mixing bowl until pale and fluffy. Add the polenta and continue to beat until combined and beat in the eggs, a little at a time.

Sift in the flour and baking powder, and then fold in quickly until blended. The mixture will be slightly lumpy.

Stir in the milk to loosen, then gently fold in the cherries.

Spoon the mixture into the paper cases and bake for 20 minutes until golden, risen and springy to the touch. Cool in the tins for 5 minutes, then place on a wire rack to cool completely.

To decorate, put a scoop of ice cream on each cake and quickly spread to cover the top of the cakes. Top with a cherry and sprinkle with sugar sprinkles. Serve immediately or freeze without the candied cherry and sugar sprinkles.

Chocolate frog cupcakes

Prep and cook time: 55 minutes
makes: 12

Ingredients:
300 g | 11 oz | 2 ½ cups self-raising flour
40 g | 1.5 oz | ⅓ cup cocoa powder
½ tsp bicarbonate of soda
(baking soda)
180 g | 6 oz | 1 ¼ cups caster
(superfine) sugar
375 ml | 13 fl. oz | 1 ½ cups buttermilk
2 eggs
150 g | 5 oz | ¾ cup butter, melted

For the icing:
110 g | 4 oz | ½ cup unsalted butter
175 g | 6 oz | 1 ¼ cups chocolate chips

For the white coconut balls:
200 ml | 7 fl. oz | ⅞ cup cream
200 g | 7 oz | 3 cups white
chocolate, chopped
200 g | 7 oz | 3 cups desiccated
(shredded) coconut

To decorate:
12 black liquorice candies, halved
110 g | 4 oz | ½ cup white chocolate

Method:
For the cupcakes, heat the oven to 200°C (175° fan) 400F, gas 6. Place 12 paper cupcake cases in a bun tin.

Sift the flour, cocoa and bicarbonate of soda into a mixing bowl. Stir in the sugar. Whisk the buttermilk with the eggs and pour into the dry ingredients. Add the melted butter and fold in gently until just combined.

Spoon the mixture into the cases and bake for 20-25 minutes until risen and springy to the touch. Remove from the tin and cool on a wire rack.

For the icing, melt the butter and chocolate chips in a small pan over a low heat. Remove from the heat and leave it to cool. Decorate the cupcakes with the icing.

For the white coconut balls, heat the cream in a pan to boiling point. Immediately remove from the heat and add the chocolate. When the chocolate has melted, stir once and chill for 2 hours until firm. Scoop out teaspoons of the mixture and roll into 24 walnut sized balls. Sprinkle the coconut on a plate and roll the balls in the coconut. Place 2 balls on each cupcake and press half a liquorice candy into each.

To decorate, melt the white chocolate in a bowl over a pan of simmering (not boiling) water. Place a small amount of the cooled white chocolate on the cupcake, to create a mouth, and leave to set.

Mini cupcakes with cream

Prep and cook time: 40 minutes
makes: 24

Ingredients:
110 g | 4 oz | ½ cup butter
110 g | 4 oz | ½ cup caster
(superfine) sugar
2 eggs, beaten
110 g | 4 oz | 1 cup self-raising flour
1 tsp vanilla extract

For the cream:
3 tbsp plain (all-purpose) flour
110 ml | 4 oz milk
110 g | 4 oz | ½ cup butter
110 g | 4 oz | ½ cup sugar
1 tsp vanilla extract
pink food dye
green food dye

To decorate:
sugar flowers
jelly candies
pastel coloured candies
sprinkles

Method:
For the cupcakes, heat the oven to 180°C (155° fan) 350F,
gas 4 and place paper cases in a small 24 hole bun tin.

Beat the butter and sugar until light and creamy, then
gradually beat in the eggs until well blended. Sift in the
flour and fold in gently with the vanilla, until just combined.

Spoon the mixture into the paper cases and bake for
10-15 minutes until golden and springy to the touch.
Place on a wire rack to cool completely.

For the icing, whisk together the flour and milk, in a small pan
over medium heat. Whisk continuously until it starts to thicken.
Continue whisking until thick. Remove the pan from the heat
and leave to cool completely.

Beat the butter and the sugar with an electric whisk until
smooth and fluffy. Gradually whisk in the thickened milk mixture
and the vanilla. Continue whisking until thick and very smooth,
for roughly 5 minutes. Divide the mixture between 3 small bowls.
Add green food dye to a bowl and pink to another, leaving the
final bowl plain.

Spoon the icing into small piping bags and pipe swirls onto
the top of the cupcakes. Decorate with sugar flowers, candies,
sprinkles and vanilla seeds as desired.

Lemon cupcakes

Prep and cook time: 40 minutes
makes: 12

Ingredients:
110 g | 4 oz | ½ cup butter
110 g | 4 oz | ½ cup caster
(superfine) sugar
1 lemon, grated zest
2 eggs, beaten
75 ml | 2 ½ fl. oz | ⅓ cup milk
150 g | 5 oz | 1 ¼ cups plain
(all-purpose) flour
1 tsp baking powder
a pinch of salt

For the icing:
225 g | 8 oz | 1 cup unsalted butter
450 g | 1 lb | 3 cups icing
(confectioners') sugar
4-5 tbsp lemon curd
yellow food dye
2 lemons, grated zest

Method:
Preheat the oven to 190°C (170° fan) 325F, gas 5 and place
12 paper cases in a cupcake tin.

Beat the butter and sugar until light and fluffy. Beat in the
lemon zest, eggs and milk, a little at a time until combined.
Sift in the flour and baking powder and gently fold into the
mixture with the salt until smooth.

Spoon the mixture into the paper cases and bake for
20 minutes until golden and springy to the touch.
Place the cupcakes on a wire rack to cool.

For the icing, beat the butter until creamy, then gradually
sift in the icing sugar and beat until smooth. Stir in the lemon
curd and a few drops of yellow food dye. Spoon or pipe the
buttercream on top of the cakes and sprinkle with lemon zest.

Gingerbread men cupcakes

Prep and cook time: 45 minutes
makes: 12

Ingredients:
175 g | 6 oz | ¾ cup butter
175 g | 6 oz | ¾ cup sugar
3 eggs, beaten
60 ml | 2 fl. oz golden syrup
225 g | 8 oz | 2 cups self-raising flour
2 tsp ground ginger
1 ½ tbsp ground almonds
1-2 tbsp milk

To decorate:
350 g | 12 oz | 2 ½ cups icing
(confectioners') sugar
45 ml | 1 ½ fl. oz lemon juice
1-2 tsp water
225 g | 8 oz brown sugar paste
1 tube decorating icing, black

Method:
For the cupcakes, preheat the oven to 180°C (160° fan) 350F, gas 4 and place 12 cupcake cases in a cupcake tin.

Beat the butter and sugar in a mixing bowl until soft and creamy, then gradually beat in the eggs. Stir in the golden syrup.

Sift in the flour and ground ginger and gently stir until combined. Stir in the ground almonds and milk until smooth.

Spoon the mixture into the cases and bake for 20 minutes until golden and springy to the touch. Remove the cakes from the tin and place on a wire rack to cool.

For the icing, sift the icing sugar into a bowl and gradually stir in the lemon juice and water until the mixture is smooth and thick. Spread the icing on top of each cake.

To decorate, roll out the sugarpaste and cut out 12 figures using a small gingerbread figure cutter. Alternatively, draw out your own figures using a toothpick. Dampen the figures slightly with water and place on top of the cakes. Pipe on eyes and mouths using the decorating icing.

Pink fairy cakes

Prep and cook time: 35 minutes
makes: 12

Ingredients:
110 g | 4 oz | ½ cup butter
110 g | 4 oz | ½ cup caster
(superfine) sugar
2 eggs
120 g | 4 ½ oz self-raising flour
25 g | 1 oz | ⅕ cup ground almonds
½ tsp almond extract

To decorate:
200 g | 7 oz | 1 ½ cups icing
(confectioners') sugar
1-2 tbsp hot water
pink food dye
pink sparkling sugar crystals
white sugar hearts
pink sugar stars

Method:
For the cupcakes, heat the oven to 180°C (160° fan) 350F, gas 4. Place 12 paper cases in a cupcake tin.

Put the butter, sugar, eggs, flour and baking powder into a mixing bowl and beat with an electric whisk for 1-2 minutes until the mixture is light and combined. Lightly fold in the ground almonds and almond extract.

Spoon the mixture into the paper cases and bake for 20 minutes until risen and golden. Leave the cakes to cool in the tins for 5 minutes, then place on a wire rack to cool.

For the icing, sift the icing sugar into a bowl and gradually stir in the hot water until smooth and thick. Stir in a few drops of food dye.

Spoon the icing on the cakes, allowing it to trickle down the sides. Sprinkle with the sugar crystals and decorate with sugar hearts and stars before the icing sets.

Yoghurt cupcakes

Prep and cook time: 45 minutes
makes: 12

Ingredients:
75 g | 2 ½ oz butter, melted
1 egg, beaten
175 ml | 6 fl. oz | ¾ cup plain yoghurt
3 limes, juice and grated zest
250 g | 9 oz | 2 ¼ cups plain
(all-purpose) flour
1 tbsp baking powder
150 g | 5 oz sugar

To decorate:
140 g | 5 oz butter
250 g | 1 ½ cups icing
(confectioners') sugar
1-2 tbsp milk
yellow, orange and green food dyes
110 g | 4 oz icing (confectioners') sugar
1 egg white, lightly beaten
yellow, orange and green sparkling
sugar crystals

Method:
For the cupcakes, heat the oven to 180°C (160° fan) 350F, gas 4. Place 12 paper cases in a cupcake tin.

Mix together the butter, egg, yoghurt, lime juice and zest. Stir together the flour, baking powder and sugar in a mixing bowl. Add the egg mixture and stir until blended.

Spoon the mixture into the paper cases and bake for 20-25 minutes until golden and springy to the touch. Remove from the tin and place on a wire rack to cool.

For the buttercream, beat the butter in a bowl until soft. Sift in half of the icing sugar and beat until smooth. Add the remaining icing sugar and one tablespoon of the milk and beat the mixture until it is creamy and smooth. Beat in more milk, if necessary, to loosen the mixture.

Divide the mixture evenly between 3 bowls. Add a few drops of green food dye to a bowl, orange food dye to another and the yellow food dye to the final bowl. Spread the buttercream over the cakes.

For the icing, sift the icing sugar into a bowl and beat in a little egg white at a time, to make a smooth icing that is thick enough to pipe. Put the icing into a piping bag and pipe lines and dots on top of the buttercream.

Press sparkling sugar crystals around the edges of the cakes.

Sparkly pink fairy cakes

Prep and cook time: 50 minutes
makes: 12

Ingredients:
2 eggs
110 g | 4 oz | 1 cup self-raising flour
50 g | 2 oz | ⅓ cup ground almonds
1 tsp baking powder
110 g | 4 oz | ½ cup butter, softened
110 g | 4 oz | ½ cup sugar
½ tsp almond extract
1 tbsp milk

To decorate:
250 g | 9 oz | 1 ½ cups icing
(confectioners') sugar
2-3 tbsp hot water
½ tsp almond extract
pink food dye
350 g | 12 oz pink sugarpaste
110 g | 4 oz yellow marzipan
1 tsp vanilla seeds
pink sparkling sugar

Method:

For the cupcakes, heat the oven to 190°C (170° fan) 400F, gas 5 and place paper cases in a 12 hole bun tin.

Put all the cake ingredients in a mixing bowl and beat well until smooth.

Spoon the mixture into the paper cases and bake for 15-20 minutes until golden and springy to the touch. Remove from the tin and place on a wire rack to cool completely.

For the icing, sift the icing sugar into a bowl and beat in enough water to give a smooth thick icing. Stir in the almond extract and food dye until smooth.

Spoon the icing onto the cakes, reserving a little to attach the flowers, and sprinkle with sparkling sugar crystals.

To make the flowers, roll out the sugarpaste and cut out individual petals. Attach the flowers to the cakes with a little icing.

Knead the marzipan with the vanilla seeds. Roll small pieces of marzipan into tiny balls and place a ball in the centre of each flower and on the cakes. Sprinkle with more sparkling sugar.

Coconut and chocolate cupcakes

Prep and cook time: 55 minutes
makes: 12

Ingredients:
175 g | 6 oz | ¾ cup butter
200 g | 7 oz | 1 cup caster
(superfine) sugar
1 tsp vanilla extract
225 g | 8 oz | 2 cups plain
(all-purpose) flour
2 tsp baking powder
125 ml | 4 fl. oz | ½ cup natural
(plain) yoghurt
175 g | 6 oz | 2 cups desiccated
(flaked) coconut

To decorate:
175 g | 6 oz | 1 ¼ cups icing
(confectioners') sugar
1 tbsp hot water
75 g | 2 ½ oz | 1 cup sweetened
flaked coconut
red and white chocolate beans

Method:
For the cupcakes, heat the oven to 180°C (155° fan), 350F, gas 4 and place paper cases in a 12 hole cupcake tin.

Cream the butter and sugar in a mixing bowl until soft and light. Beat in the eggs, one at a time, then stir in the vanilla. Sift in the flour and baking powder and stir until incorporated. Add the yoghurt and coconut and stir until blended.

Spoon the mixture into the paper cases and bake for 25-30 minutes until golden and springy to the touch. Cool in the tin for 10 minutes, then place on a wire rack to cool completely.

For the decoration, sift the icing sugar into a bowl and gradually stir in the hot water until the mixture is the consistency of cream.

Spread a thin layer on top of each cake and sprinkle with coconut. Place a few chocolate beans on top of each cake.

Lime cupcakes

Prep and cook time: 40 minutes
makes: 12

Ingredients:
2 eggs
110 g | 4 oz | 1 cup self-raising flour
½ tsp baking powder
110 g | 4 oz | ½ cup butter, softened
110 g | 4 oz | ½ cup sugar
1 lime, juice and zest

To decorate:
140 g | 5 oz unsalted butter
250 g | 9 oz | 2 ¼ cups icing
(confectioners') sugar
2-3 tbsp lime juice
green food dye
24 mini fruit jelly slices
white sugar sprinkles

Method:
For the cupcakes, heat the oven to 180°C (160° fan) 350F, gas 4. Place 12 paper cases in a cupcake tin.

Beat the butter and sugar in a mixing bowl until light and creamy. Add the eggs gradually, beating well. Add the juice and zest of one lime, then sift in the flour and baking powder and gently fold into the mixture.

Spoon the mixture into the paper cases and bake for about 20 minutes, until golden and springy to the touch. Remove from the tin and place on a wire rack to cool.

For the buttercream, beat the butter until soft and creamy. Sift in the icing sugar and beat well. Stir in the vanilla and food dye.

Whisk with an electric whisk for 5-10 minutes. Reduce the speed to low and gradually whisk in the lime juice until it reaches the right consistency for piping.

Put the buttercream into a piping bag and pipe a swirl on top of the cakes. Put a spoonful of the icing in the centre and place 2 mini jelly slices on each cake.

Banana cupcakes

Prep and cook time: 45 minutes
makes: 12

Ingredients:
200 g | 7 oz | 1 ¾ cups plain (all-purpose) flour
100 g | 3 ½ oz fine oatmeal
½ tsp lemon zest
2 tsp baking powder
½ tsp bicarbonate of soda (baking soda)
1 egg
120 g | 4 ½ oz sugar
50 ml | 2 fl. oz vegetable oil
2 ripe bananas
30 ml | 1 fl. oz lemon juice
120 ml | 4 fl. oz | ½ cup buttermilk

To decorate:
200 ml | 7 fl.oz | ⅞ cup cream
75 g | 2 ½ oz candy coated chocolate
12 edible decorations (optional, such as the one shown)

Method:
Preheat the oven to 180°C (160° fan) 350F, gas 4. Place 12 paper cases in a cupcake tin.

Combine the flour with the oatmeal, lemon zest, baking powder and bicarbonate of soda in a bowl.

Whisk together the egg, sugar and oil and stir into the flour mixture until combined. Mash the bananas with the lemon juice and buttermilk. Stir into the mixing bowl until blended.

Spoon the mixture into the paper cases and bake for 25-30 minutes until golden and springy to the touch. Allow the cakes to cool in the tin for 10 minutes, then transfer to a wire rack to cool completely.

To decorate, whisk the cream until it forms firm peaks and place a spoonful on top of each cupcake. Decorate with the candy coated chocolate and an edible decoration, if desired.

Butterfly cupcakes

Prep and cook time: 50 minutes
makes: 12

Ingredients:
2 eggs
110 g | 4 oz | 1 cup self-raising flour
½ tsp baking powder
110 g | 4 oz | ½ cup butter, softened
110 g | 4 oz | ½ cup sugar

To decorate:
110 g | 4 oz | ½ cup butter
225 g | 8 oz | 1 ¾ cups icing
(confectioners') sugar
½ tsp vanilla extract
green food dye
32 assorted mini fruit jelly slices
24 assorted chewy fruit candies

Method:
Heat the oven to 170°C (150° fan), 325F, gas 3 and place paper cases in a 12 hole bun tin.

Put all of the cupcake ingredients into a mixing bowl and whisk until well combined.

Spoon the mixture into the paper cases and bake for 20-25 minutes until golden and springy to the touch. Remove from the tin and place on a wire rack to cool.

To decorate, beat the butter until soft and creamy. Sift in the icing sugar and beat well. Stir in the vanilla. Put half the buttercream into a small bowl and stir in a few drops of green food dye.

Spread the buttercream over the top of the cooled cupcakes, 6 green and 6 plain. Place 2 fruit jelly slices on each cake to form wings.

Cut the remaining fruit jelly slices into 3 and roll between your hands to form the body shapes. Use 2 contrasting colours to form the body and place between the fruit jelly slices. Add 2 fruit candies to each cake for the butterfly feelers.

Chocolate chip cupcakes

Prep and cook time: 45 minutes
makes: 12

Ingredients:
110 g | 4 oz | ½ cup butter
75 g | 2 ½ oz sugar
30 g | 1 oz light brown sugar
2 eggs, beaten
175 g | 6 oz | 1 ½ cups plain
(all-purpose) flour
1 tsp baking powder
110 ml | 4 oz | milk
½ tsp vanilla extract
75 g | 2 ½ oz | ½ cup chocolate chips

For the buttercream:
140 g | 5 oz butter
300 g | 10 ½ oz | 2 cups icing
(confectioners') sugar
1 tbsp milk
75 g | 2 ½ oz chocolate, melted
50 g | 2 oz white chocolate,
coarsely grated

Method:
For the cupcakes, heat the oven to 190°C (170° fan) 400F, gas 5. Place 12 paper cases in a cupcake tin.

Beat the butter and both sugars until light and fluffy. Beat in the eggs, a little at a time, mixing well.

Sift the flour and baking powder into the mixture and fold in gently with the milk and vanilla. Gently stir in the chocolate chips.

Spoon the mixture into the paper cases and bake for 20-25 minutes until golden and risen. Leave the cupcakes in the tins for 5 minutes, then place on a wire rack to cool.

For the buttercream, beat the butter in a bowl until soft. Sift in the icing sugar and beat until smooth. Beat in the melted chocolate until creamy and smooth. Chill until the mixture has become firm enough to pipe.

Spoon the buttercream into a piping bag and pipe swirls, or stars on top of each cake. Sprinkle with grated white chocolate to decorate.

Party fun cupcakes

Prep and cook time: 50 minutes
makes: 12

Ingredients:
225 g | 8 oz | 2 cups plain
(all-purpose) flour
100 g | 3 ½ oz | ½ cup caster
(superfine) sugar
2 tsp baking powder
a pinch of salt
1 egg, beaten
150 ml | 5 oz | ⅔ cup milk
50 g | 2 oz | ¼ cup butter, melted
1 tsp vanilla extract

To decorate:
225 g | 8 oz | 1 ½ cups icing
(confectioners') sugar
2-3 tbsp hot water
2-3 tsp cocoa powder
food dyes, red, green, blue

To decorate:
chocolate beans
chocolate kisses
chocolate buttons
liquorice sticks
chocolate sprinkles
assorted candies
red piping icing
sparkling sugar

Method:
For the cupcakes, heat the oven to 190°C (170° fan) 400F, gas 5.
Place 12 paper cases in a cupcake tin.

Sift the flour, sugar, baking powder and salt into a mixing bowl.
Whisk together the egg, milk, butter and vanilla. Stir into the dry
ingredients until combined.

Spoon the mixture into the paper cases and bake for 20 minutes
until golden and risen. Cool in the tin for 5 minutes then place
the cupcakes on a wire rack to cool.

For the icing, sift the icing sugar into a bowl and beat in the
hot water until smooth.

Divide the mixture into smaller bowls and stir a few drops of
your chosen food dye into each bowl. For the chocolate icing,
sift in the cocoa powder to a bowl and beat well.

Spread the icing over the cakes and add the decorations
before the icing sets. See these cupcakes for inspiration.

Cupcakes with hundreds and thousands

Prep and cook time: 40 minutes
makes: 12

Ingredients:
225 g | 8 oz | 1 cup unsalted butter
225 g | 8 oz | 1 cup caster
(superfine) sugar
4 eggs, beaten
50 g | 2 oz | ½ cup plain
(all-purpose) flour
150 g | 5 oz | 1 ¼ cups ground almonds
1 tsp vanilla extract
1 tbsp milk

To decorate:
300 ml | 10 fl. oz | 1 ⅓ cups cream
1 tbsp icing (confectioners')
sugar, sifted
vanilla extract
sugar sprinkles

Method:

For the cupcakes, heat the oven to 180°C (155° fan), 350F, gas 4 and place paper cases in a 12 hole bun tin.

Beat the butter and sugar until light and fluffy. Gradually beat in the eggs until blended.

Sift in the flour, then add the ground almonds, vanilla and milk and stir well.

Spoon the mixture into the paper cases and bake for 20-25 minutes until golden and springy to the touch.

Cool in the tins for 5 minutes, then place on a wire rack to cool completely.

For the decoration, whisk the cream, icing sugar and a few drops of vanilla until thick. Spoon the mixture into a piping bag and pipe swirls on top of each cake. Scatter with sugar sprinkles just before serving.

Banana bee muffins

Prep and cook time: 40 minutes
makes: 12

Ingredients:
250 g | 9 oz | 2 ½ cups self-raising flour
2 tbsp light brown sugar
50 g | 2 oz | ¼ cup butter, melted
2 small ripe bananas, mashed
2 eggs, beaten
30 ml | 1 fl. oz clear honey
75 ml | 2 ½ fl. oz milk

To decorate:
225 g | 8 oz yellow sugarpaste
2 tubes brown piping gel
24 flaked almonds
45 ml | 1 ½ fl. oz clear honey

Method:
Preheat the oven to 190°C (170° fan) 375F, gas 5. Place 12 paper cases in a cupcake tin.

Put the flour, sugar, butter and bananas in a bowl and mix together until combined. Whisk together the eggs, honey and milk and stir into the other ingredients until just blended.

Spoon the mixture into the paper cases, filling almost to the top.

Bake for 15-20 minutes until risen and firm to the touch. Gently warm the honey and spoon over the cooled cakes.

For the bees, divide the sugarpaste into 12 equal pieces. Break off a small piece from each and set aside for the heads. Roll the remaining larger pieces between your palms to form the body shapes. Roll the smaller pieces into balls. Place the bodies on the muffins and attach the heads with a dab of honey.

Pipe stripes on the bodies and faces on the heads with brown piping gel. Attach 2 flaked almonds to each body to form the wings.

Party cupcakes

Prep and cook time: 35 minutes
makes: 12

Ingredients:
110 g | 4 oz | ½ cup unsalted butter
110 g | 4 oz | ½ cup caster sugar
½ tsp vanilla extract
2 eggs, beaten
140 g | 5 oz | 1 ¼ cups self-raising flour

To decorate:
250 g | 9 oz | 1 ⅛ cups unsalted butter
400 g | 14 oz | 2 ⅓ cups icing sugar
1 orange, juiced and grated zest
12 orange jelly starfish
3-4 tbsp coarse sugar crystals

Method:
Preheat the oven to 180°C (160° fan) 350F, gas 4. Line a 12 hole cupcake tin with paper cases.

Cream the butter and the sugar together until light and fluffy. Add the vanilla, followed by the eggs. Slowly fold in the flour until combined and spoon the mixture into the paper cases.

Bake for 10-15 minutes until risen and springy to the touch. Remove the cakes from the tin and cool on a wire rack.

For the buttercream, beat the butter until soft and creamy. Sift in the icing sugar and beat well. Gradually beat in sufficient orange juice to give a soft spreading consistency and stir in the zest.

Spoon the buttercream thickly on top of each cake. Place a jelly starfish in the centre of each cake and sprinkle with sugar crystals.

Chocolate marshmallow cupcakes

Prep and cook time: 35 minutes
makes: 12

Ingredients:
150 g | 5 oz butter
300 g | 10 oz | 1 ½ cups caster
(superfine) sugar
3 eggs, beaten
250 ml | 8 ½ fl. oz | 1 cup milk
225 g | 8 oz | 2 cups plain
(all-purpose) flour
a pinch of salt
1 tsp bicarbonate of soda
(baking soda)
50 g | 2 oz | ½ cup cocoa powder

For the icing:
110 g | 4 oz dark (plain) chocolate
150 g | 5 oz butter
160 g | 1 ⅓ cups icing (confectioners')
sugar, sifted
1 tsp vanilla extract

To decorate:
110 g | 4 oz dark (plain) chocolate,
roughly chopped
110 g | 4 oz walnuts, chopped
mini marshmallows

Method:
Preheat the oven to 180°C (155° fan), 350F, gas 4 and place paper cases in a 12 hole bun tin.

Beat the butter and sugar in a mixing bowl until soft and creamy. Beat in the eggs and milk, then sift in the flour, salt, bicarbonate of soda and cocoa and combine until smooth.

Spoon the mixture into the paper cases. Bake for 12-15 minutes, until the cupcakes are golden and springy to the touch. Remove from the tin and cool on a wire rack.

For the chocolate icing, melt the chocolate in a heatproof bowl over a pan of simmering water. Remove from the heat and cool for 5 minutes. Beat the butter with an electric whisk until smooth and creamy.

Add the sugar and beat until light and fluffy. Beat in the vanilla and melted chocolate on a low speed until smooth. Increase the speed and beat until the mixture is glossy.

Spread the icing on the cooled cupcakes and decorate with chopped chocolate, walnuts and mini marshmallows.

index.

Advocaat
  Advocaat cupcakes 40
almond extract
  Easter cupcakes 128
  Mini cherry cupcakes 28
  Sparkly pink fairy cakes 198
almonds
  Chocolate Christmas cupcakes 136
  Gingerbread cupcakes 160
almonds, flaked
  Banana bee muffins 214
  Bee sting cupcakes 50
almonds, ground
  Carrot cupcakes 162
  Cupcakes with hundreds and thousands 212
  Easter cupcakes 128
  Fairy cakes 96
  Gingerbread men cupcakes 192
  Halloween cupcakes 144
  Sparkly pink fairy cakes 198
  Raspberry bun cupcakes 108
  Snowmen cupcakes 118
  Vanilla and chocolate cupcakes 78
apple
  Apple cupcakes 86
apricot jam
  Easter cupcakes 128
  Snowmen cupcakes 118
  Spider cupcakes 148
  Sugar flower cupcakes 70

bananas
  Banana bee muffins 214
  Banana cupcakes 102, 204
black treacle
  Halloween cupcakes 144
buttermilk
  Banana cupcakes 204
  Chocolate frog cupcakes 186
  Red velvet cupcakes 82

candies, candy heart
  Candy heart cupcakes 154
candies, chocolate
  Caterpillar cupcakes 178
  Cupcakes with candy-coated chocolate 168
  Easter cupcakes 140
  Halloween cupcakes 144
  Mini cupcakes with coloured cream 188
  Noughts and crosses cupcakes 182
  Party fun cupcakes 210

candies, coated chocolate
  Banana cupcakes 204
  Coconut and chocolate cupcakes 200
  Halloween cupcakes 144
  Noughts and crosses cupcakes 182
candies, fruit
  Butterfly cupcakes 206
  Pink-iced chocolate cupcakes 180
candies, jelly
  Frankenstein cupcakes 126
  Mini cupcakes with coloured cream 188
  Monster cupcakes 172
  Party cupcakes 216
candies, liquorice
  Caterpillar cupcakes 178
  Chocolate frog cupcakes 186
  Monster cupcakes 172
  Party fun cupcakes 210
  Skeleton cupcakes 152
  Spider cupcakes 148
candies, strawberry laces
  Caterpillar cupcakes 178
  Snowmen cupcakes 118
cardamom, ground
  Chocolate Christmas cupcakes 136
carrot
  Carrot cupcakes 60, 162
cherries
  Mini cherry cupcakes 28
cherries, glacé
  Ice-cream cupcakes 184
  Mini cherry cupcakes 28
  Vanilla cupcakes 80
cherry compote
  Black Forest cupcakes 30
chocolate, dark
  Advocaat cupcakes 40
  Birthday cupcakes 124
  Black Forest cupcakes 30
  Boston cream cupcakes 20
  Candy heart cupcakes 154
  Chocolate Christmas cupcakes 114
  Chocolate cupcakes 36, 56
  Chocolate cupcakes with sugar pearls 62
  Chocolate ganache cupcakes 46
  Chocolate ginger cupcakes 16
  Chocolate marshmallow cupcakes 218
  Chocolate meringue cupcakes 26
  Chocolate raspberry cupcakes 74, 110
  Chocolate sauce cupcakes 46
  Christmas cupcakes 132
  Giant cream cupcakes 10

Hazelnut fancy cupcakes 54
  Monster cupcakes 172
  Skeleton cupcakes 152
  Spider cupcakes 148
  Valentine's Day chocolate cupcakes 116
  Valentine's Day cupcakes 138
  Vanilla and chocolate cupcakes 78
  Vanilla-iced chocolate cupcakes 18
chocolate, milk
  Chocolate chip cupcakes 208
  Chocolate cupcakes with sugar pearls 62
  Hazelnut fancy cupcakes 54
  Vanilla chocolate cupcakes 170
chocolate, white
  Chocolate chip cupcakes 208
  Chocolate cupcakes with sugar pearls 62
  Christmas cupcakes 132
  Chocolate frog cupcakes 186
  Vanilla cream cupcakes 100
chocolate chips
  Chocolate chip cupcakes 208
  Chocolate frog cupcakes 186
  Valentine's Day chocolate cupcakes 116
  Valentine's Day cupcakes 138
chocolate hazelnut spread
  Hazelnut fancy cupcakes 54
chocolate marshmallow biscuits
  Spider cupcakes 148
cinnamon, ground
  Carrot cupcakes 60
  Chocolate Christmas cupcakes 136
  Chocolate ganache cupcakes 46
  Chocolate strawberry cream cakes 104
  Christmas cupcakes with silver balls 122
  Cinnamon Christmas cupcakes 132
  Hazelnut cinnamon cupcakes 122
  Independence Day cupcakes 130
  Chocolate ginger cupcakes 16
  Rum and ginger cupcakes 12
  Gingerbread cupcakes 160
  Mince pie cupcakes 156
  Pumpkin cupcakes 158
clementine
  Clementine cupcakes 120
  Reindeer cupcakes 146
cloves, ground
  Chocolate Christmas cupcakes 136
  Gingerbread cupcakes 160
  Pumpkin cupcakes 158
cocoa powder
  Advocaat cupcakes 40

Black Forest cupcakes 30
Candy heart cupcakes 154
Chocolate Christmas cupcakes 114, 136
Chocolate cupcakes 36, 176
Chocolate frog cupcakes 186
Chocolate ginger cupcakes 16
Chocolate marshmallow cupcakes 218
Chocolate meringue cupcakes 26
Chocolate raspberry cupcakes 74
Chocolate strawberry cream cakes 104
Cinnamon Christmas cupcakes 132
Monster cupcakes 172
Nougat Christmas cupcakes 134
Party fun cupcakes 210
Pink-iced chocolate cupcakes 180
Red velvet cupcakes 82
Spider cupcakes 148
Star spangled cupcakes 142
Tiramisu cupcakes 34
Valentine's Day chocolate cupcakes 116
Valentine's Day cupcakes 138
Vanilla-iced chocolate cupcakes 18
coconut, desiccated
  Chocolate frog cupcakes 186
  Coconut and chocolate cupcakes 200
  Coconut cupcakes 52
  Iced fairy cakes 98
coffee, espresso
  Espresso cupcakes with mascarpone cream 42
coffee powder, espresso
  Tiramisu cupcakes 34
condensed milk
  Cupcakes with ice-cream 22
courgette
  Chocolate cupcakes 56
cream
  Advocaat cupcakes 40
  Banana cupcakes 102, 204
  Bee sting cupcakes 50
  Black Forest cupcakes 30
  Boston cream cupcakes 20
  Buttercream cupcakes 64
  Butterfly buns 76
  Chocolate Christmas cupcakes 114
  Chocolate cupcakes 36, 176
  Chocolate cupcakes with sugar pearls 62
  Chocolate frog cupcakes 186
  Chocolate ganache cupcakes 46
  Chocolate ginger cupcakes 16
  Chocolate raspberry cupcakes 110
  Chocolate sauce cupcakes 46

Chocolate strawberry cream cakes 104
Cinnamon Christmas cupcakes 132
Cupcakes with hundreds and thousands 212
Cupcakes with pink icing 68
Birthday cupcakes 124
Cupcakes with sugar flowers 90
Easter cupcakes 140
Giant cream cupcakes 10
Halloween cupcakes 144
Hazelnut fancy cupcakes 54
Mince pie cupcakes 156
Monster cupcakes 172
Nougat Christmas cupcakes 134
Noughts and crosses cupcakes 182
Pink-iced chocolate cupcakes 180
Raspberry bun cupcakes 108
Strawberry cupcakes 44
Tiramisu cupcakes 34
Toffee cupcakes 24
Valentine's Day cupcakes 138
Vanilla-iced chocolate cupcakes 18
cream, clotted
  Carrot cupcakes 60
cream, soured
  Candy heart cupcakes 154
  Cupcakes with candy coated chocolate 168
cream cheese
  Banana cupcakes 102
  Carrot cupcakes 162
  Red velvet cupcakes 82
crème fraiche
  Cupcakes with pink buttercream 92
  Lemon cupcakes 94
  Noughts and crosses cupcakes 182
  Raspberry bun cupcakes 108
  Skeleton cupcakes 152

eggs
  Boston cream cupcakes 20
  Carrot cupcakes 162
  Chocolate meringue cupcakes 26
  Meringue cupcakes 8

figs
  Rum and ginger cupcakes 12
  fondant icing, ready-to-roll
  Halloween cupcakes 144
  Snowmen cupcakes 118
food dye, blue
  Buttercream cupcakes 64
  Frankenstein cupcakes 126

Noughts and crosses cupcakes 182
Party fun cupcakes 210
Sugar flower cupcakes 70
food dye, green
  Butterfly cupcakes 206
  Chocolate Christmas cupcakes 136
  Cupcakes with sugar flowers 90
  Easter cupcakes 128
  Frankenstein cupcakes 126
  Lime cupcakes 202
  Mince pie cupcakes 156
  Mini cupcakes with coloured cream 188
  Party fun cupcakes 210
  Yoghurt cupcakes 196
food dye, lilac
  Fairy cakes 174
food dye, orange
  Easter cupcakes 128
  Frankenstein cupcakes 126
  Pumpkin cupcakes 158
  Sports balls cupcakes 166
  Yoghurt cupcakes 196
food dye, pink
  Buttercream cupcakes 64
  Cupcakes with pink buttercream 92
  Cupcakes with pink icing 68
  Cupcakes with sugar flowers 90
  Fairy cakes 88, 96
  Iced fairy cakes 98
  Macadamia nut cupcakes 38
  Mini cupcakes with coloured cream 188
  Sparkly pink fairy cakes 198
  Pink-iced chocolate cupcakes 180
  Tea time cupcakes 84

food dye, red
  Chocolate Christmas cupcakes 136
  Cinnamon Christmas cupcakes 132
  Mince pie cupcakes 156
  Party fun cupcakes 210
  Red velvet cupcakes 82
food dye, yellow
  Candy heart cupcakes 154
  Lemon cupcakes 94, 190
  Pumpkin cupcakes 158
  Sugar flower cupcakes 70
  Yoghurt cupcakes 196
Frangelico hazelnut liquor
  Hazelnut fancy cupcakes 54

ginger, crystallized
  Chocolate ginger cupcakes 16

index.

ginger, ground
  Cinnamon Christmas cupcakes 132
  Ginger chocolate cupcakes 16
  Gingerbread cupcakes 160
  Gingerbread men cupcakes 192
  Halloween cupcakes 144
  Pumpkin cupcakes 158
ginger, root
  Rum and ginger cupcakes 12
ginger, stem
  Chocolate ginger cupcakes 16
  Gingerbread cupcakes 160
ginger, syrup
  Gingerbread cupcakes 160
golden syrup
  Gingerbread men cupcakes 192
  Rum and ginger cupcakes 12

hazelnuts
  Hazelnut fancy cupcakes 54
hazelnuts, ground
  Chocolate meringue cupcakes 26
  Christmas cupcakes with silver balls 122
  Hazelnut fancy cupcakes 54
honey
  Banana bee muffins 214
  Bee sting cupcakes 50
  Chocolate Christmas cupcakes 136
  Gingerbread cupcakes 160

Ice-cream, raspberry ripple
  Cupcakes with ice cream 22
Ice-cream, vanilla
  Cupcakes with ice cream 22
  Ice-cream cupcakes 184
  Ice-cream cupcakes 32
icing (confectioners) sugar
  Advocaat cupcakes 40
  Birthday cupcakes 124
  Buttercream and raspberry cupcakes 14
  Buttercream cupcakes 64
  Butterfly cupcakes 206
  Carrot cupcakes 162
  Caterpillar cupcakes 178
  Chocolate Chip cupcakes 208
  Chocolate Christmas cupcakes 136
  Chocolate cupcakes 56, 176
  Chocolate ganache cupcakes 46
  Chocolate ginger cupcakes 16
  Chocolate meringue cupcakes 26
  Chocolate raspberry cupcakes 74

Coconut and chocolate cupcakes 200
Coconut cupcakes 52
Tea time cupcakes 84
Cupcakes with hundreds and thousands 212
Cupcakes with pink buttercream 92
Cupcakes with pink icing 68
Cupcakes with sugar flowers 90
Easter cupcakes 128, 140
Espresso cupcakes with mascarpone cream 42
Fairy cakes 88, 96, 174
Frankenstein cupcakes 126
Giant cream cupcakes 10
Rum and ginger cupcakes 12
Gingerbread men cupcakes 192
Halloween cupcakes 144
Iced fairy cakes 98
Star spangled cupcakes 142
Lemon cakes 66
Lemon cupcakes 94, 190
Lime cupcakes 202
Macadamia nut cupcakes 38
Mini cherry cupcakes 28
Noughts and crosses cupcakes 182
Party cupcakes 216
Party fun cupcakes 210
Pink fairy cakes 198
Sparkly pink fairy cakes 198
Pink-iced chocolate cupcakes 180
Pumpkin cupcakes 158
Raspberry buttercream cupcakes 106
Red velvet cupcakes 82
Reindeer cupcakes 146
Sports balls cupcakes 166
Vanilla and chocolate cupcakes 78
Vanilla cream cupcakes 100
Vanilla cupcakes 150
Vanilla-iced chocolate cupcakes 18
Yoghurt cupcakes 196
icing, decorating tubes
  Frankenstein cupcakes 126
  Gingerbread men cupcakes 192
  Halloween cupcakes 144
  Reindeer cupcakes 146
  Snowmen cupcakes 118

jelly slices
  Butterfly cupcakes 206
  Lime cupcakes 202

Kirsch
  Black Forest cupcakes 30

lemon
  Banana cupcakes 204
  Buttercream cupcakes 64
  Carrot cupcakes 162
  Fairy cakes 174
  Lemon cakes 66
  Lemon cupcakes 94, 190
  Meringue cupcakes 8
  Noughts and crosses cupcakes 182
lemon curd
  Lemon cupcakes 190
lemon juice
  Cupcakes with candy coated chocolate 168
  Fairy cakes 88
  Gingerbread men cupcakes 192
  Snowmen cupcakes 118
lime
  Lime cupcakes 202
  Yoghurt cupcakes 196

macadamia nuts, chopped
  Macadamia nut cupcakes 38
marmalade, orange
  Frankenstein cupcakes 126
marshmallows
  Frankenstein cupcakes 126
  Snowmen cupcakes 118
marshmallows, mini
  Chocolate marshmallow cupcakes 218
  Halloween cupcakes 144
  Skeleton cupcakes 152
  Strawberry cupcakes 44
marzipan
  Chocolate Christmas cupcakes 136
  Cinnamon Christmas cupcakes 132, 156
  Easter cupcakes 128
  Mince pie cupcakes 156
  Sparkly pink fairy cakes 198
  Raspberry bun cupcakes 108
mascarpone
  Espresso cupcakes with mascarpone cream 42
milk
  Boston cream cupcakes 20
  Ice-cream filled cupcakes 32
  Raspberry buttercream cupcakes 106
  Vanilla cream cupcakes 100
mincemeat
  Mince pie cupcakes 156
mixed spice
  Carrot cupcakes 60
  Chocolate Christmas cupcakes 136
  Nougat Christmas cupcakes 134

nougat
   Nougat Christmas cupcakes 134
nutmeg
   Mince pie cupcakes 156

oatmeal
   Banana cupcakes 204
orange
   Carrot cupcakes 60
   Noughts and crosses cupcakes 182
   Party cupcakes 216
   Skeleton cupcakes 152
   Sports balls cupcakes 166

pecan nuts
   Clementine cupcakes 120
piping gel, brown
   Banana bee muffins 214
polenta
   Ice-cream cupcakes 184
pumpkin puree
   Pumpkin cupcakes 158

raspberries
   Buttercream and raspberry cupcakes 14
   Chocolate raspberry cupcakes 74, 110
   Cupcakes with ice-cream 22
   Ice-cream cupcakes 32
   Raspberry bun cupcakes 108
raspberry jam
   Raspberry buttercream cupcakes 106
raspberry liquor
   Raspberry bun cupcakes 108
raspberry syrup
   Pink-iced chocolate cupcakes 180
rose petals
   Chocolate cupcakes 56
rosewater
   Cupcakes with pink icing 68
rum
   Chocolate ganache cupcakes 46
   Cinnamon Christmas cupcakes 132
   Rum and ginger cupcakes 12

sherry
   Christmas cupcakes 156
silver balls, edible
   Chocolate cupcakes 36
   Christmas cupcakes with silver balls 122
   Fairy cakes 96
   Gingerbread cupcakes 160
   Snowmen cupcakes 118

strawberries
   Carrot cupcakes 162
   Chocolate strawberry cream cakes 104
   Strawberry cupcakes 44
strawberry extract
   Tea time cupcakes 84
sugar, dark brown
   Chocolate Christmas cupcakes 136
   Chocolate cupcakes with sugar pearls 62
   Pink-iced chocolate cupcakes 180
sugar, light brown
   Advocaat cupcakes 40
   Banana bee muffins 214
   Birthday cupcakes 208
   Candy heart cupcakes 154
   Chocolate Christmas cupcakes 114
   Chocolate cupcakes 36
   Chocolate raspberry cupcakes 74
   Espresso cupcakes with mascarpone cream 42
   Gingerbread cupcakes 160
   Halloween cupcakes 144
   Tiramisu cupcakes 34
   Valentine's Day cupcakes 138
sugar cones
   Cupcakes with ice-cream 22
sugar crystals
   Independence Day cupcakes 130
   Party cupcakes 216
   Pumpkin cupcakes 158
   Sparkly pink fairy cakes 198
   Valentine's Day chocolate cupcakes 116
   Yoghurt cupcakes 196
sugar flowers
   Buttercream cupcakes 64
   Cupcakes with sugar flowers 90
   Iced fairy cakes 98
   Mini cupcakes with coloured cream 188
   Raspberry buttercream cupcakes 106
sugar hearts
   Sparkly pink fairy cakes 198
   Valentine's Day chocolate cupcakes 116
sugar numbers
   Fairy cakes 174
sugar pearls
   Chocolate cupcakes with sugar pearls 62
   Cupcakes with pink buttercream 92
   Spider cupcakes 148
   Tea time cupcakes 84
sugar sprinkles
   Banana cupcakes 102

Birthday cupcakes 124
Chocolate Christmas cupcakes 114
Chocolate cupcakes 176
Cupcakes with hundreds and thousands 212
Fairy cakes 174
Ice-cream cupcakes 184
Iced fairy cakes 98
Lime cupcakes 202
Mini cupcakes with coloured cream 188
Pink-iced chocolate cupcakes 180
Tea time cupcakes 84
Vanilla and chocolate cupcakes 78
Vanilla chocolate cupcakes 170
sugar stars
   Independence Day cupcakes 130
   Sparkly pink fairy cakes 198
   Star spangled cupcakes 142
sugar strands
   Cinnamon Christmas cupcakes 132
sugarpaste
   Banana bee muffins 214
   Caterpillar cupcakes 178
   Gingerbread men cupcakes 192
   Monster cupcakes 172
   Pumpkin cupcakes 158
   Reindeer cupcakes 146
   Sparkly pink fairy cakes 198
   Sugar flower cupcakes 70
   Valentine's Day chocolate cupcakes 116
sugarpaste, brown
   Gingerbread men cupcakes 192
   Reindeer cupcakes 146
sugarpaste, cream
   Reindeer cupcakes 146
sugarpaste, green
   Monster cupcakes 172
   Pumpkin cupcakes 158
sugarpaste, pink
   Sparkly pink fairy cakes 198
sugarpaste, red
   Valentine's Day chocolate cupcakes 116
sugarpaste, white
   Caterpillar cupcakes 178
   Sugar flower cupcakes 70
sugarpaste, yellow
   Banana bee muffins 214
sunflower oil
   Candy hearts cupcakes 154
   Carrot cupcakes 60
   Chocolate cupcakes 56
   Chocolate strawberry cream cakes 104
   Cupcakes with candy-coated

index.

chocolate 168
Ice-cream filled cupcakes 32
Macadamia nut cupcakes 38
Raspberry buttercream cupcakes 106
Sugar flower cupcakes 70
Toffee cupcakes 24

vanilla extract
Black Forest cupcakes 30
Boston cream cupcakes 20
Buttercream and raspberry cupcakes 14
Candy heart cupcakes 154
Carrot cupcakes 60
Chocolate chip cupcakes 208
Chocolate raspberry cupcakes 110
Christmas cupcakes with silver balls 122
Coconut and chocolate cupcakes 200
Coconut cupcakes 52
Tea time cupcakes 84
Cupcakes with hundreds and thousands 212
Cupcakes with ice-cream 22
Cupcakes with sugar flowers 90
Easter cupcakes 140
Iced fairy cakes 98
Mini cupcakes with coloured cream 188
Spider cupcakes 148
Strawberry cupcakes 44
Sugar flower cupcakes 70
Toffee cupcakes 24
Vanilla and chocolate cupcakes 78
Vanilla chocolate cupcakes 170
Vanilla cream cupcakes 100
Vanilla cupcakes 80, 150
Vanilla-iced chocolate cupcakes 18
vanilla pod
Hazelnut fancy cupcakes 54
vegetable oil
Banana cupcakes 204
Christmas cupcakes 132

walnuts
Banana cupcakes 102
Chocolate marshmallow cupcakes 218
Chocolate raspberry cupcakes 110
Rum and ginger cupcakes 12
walnuts, ground
Rum and ginger cupcakes 12
wholemeal flour
Christmas cupcakes with silver balls 122

yoghurt
Birthday cupcakes 124
Buttercream cupcakes 64
Coconut and chocolate cupcakes 200
Coconut cupcakes 52
Lemon cakes 66
Lemon cupcakes 94
Yoghurt cupcakes 196